Signals

A book of psychological and natural, comprehensive analytical quotations, essays, and poems from an observer in our world of increasing individualism through inherited wisdom, and our inherent "personal" growing wisdom.

By DUANE HALLAS and his influences and contributors

RoseDog Books
PITTSBURGH, PENNSYLVANIA 15222

The contents of this work including, but not limited to, the accuracy of events, people, and places depicted; opinions expressed; permission to use previously published materials included; and any advice given or actions advocated are solely the responsibility of the author, who assumes all liability for said work and indemnifies the publisher against any claims stemming from publication of the work.

All Rights Reserved
Copyright © 2007 by Duane Hallas
No part of this book may be reproduced or transmitted in any form or by any means, electronic or mechanical, including photocopying, recording, or by any information storage and retrieval system without permission in writing from the author.

ISBN: 978-0-8059-8841-3
Library of Congress Control Number: 2006928938

Printed in the United States of America

First Printing

For information or to order additional books, please write:
RoseDog Books
701 Smithfield St.
Third Floor
Pittsburgh, PA 15222
U.S.A.
1-800-834-1803
Or visit our web site and
on-line bookstore at www..rosedogbookstore.com

Table of Contents

Dedication iv
Introduction..v
Signals Ascend from Within 1
Earning and Deserving Money 13
From the Womb to the Tomb (poem) 19
Rage and the Bay of Wisdom (poem) 20
Obeying Nature 21
Hide and Seek (poem)..28
Re – Cap the Crap 30
To my Lost Love (poem) 34
The Bridge of Time (poem) 35
About Buckminster Fuller 36
Excerpts from Buckminster Fuller Books 46
Signals from Within 52
Thoughts on Time Travel and Our Objectives toward Space 64
God? 70
To my Friend, Mind (poem) 72
Other Statements 74
Definitions of Select Words 79
Bibliography 86

Dedication

This book is dedicated to all people with considerate and companionate awareness and actions. Having evolved consciousness of our choice of our behaviors, we morally select out of a spectrum of behaviors from our unconscious past. We try to demonstrate those legitimate behaviors to others to the best of our abilities, hoping they will realize that the "human environment," survival of the fittest scenario in which we live is neither the path for our continuance, nor for our success.

To all these people I either know or don't know, who act legitimately, I say to them, "Let us always be friends on the frequencies of good vibrations possessed by only a few in our harsh environment of unrealistic, rigid, and myopic social expectations."

This book is also dedicated to my brother, Daryl. He is included in the first part of this dedication but has shown me support when it was hard to find without trying to redirect my course.

I do have some who support me, and I don't expect anyone to agree with me, but I give special thanks to my brother for sticking by me.

I also want to thank whoever reads this book.

Life is a beautiful thing, but very intense for me.

Introduction

This book is divided into two sections: "Signals Ascend from Within" and "Signals from Within."

"Signals Ascend from Within" contains dialogue describing my opinions formed from my experiences and observations of the psychologies of people and the societies in which they are included or that they control. I've spent many a year comprehensively analyzing my social environment and I was compelled to write about it. I started with a word here, a line there. It took quite a bit of time for my explanations to "ascend" from the inventory of experiences and observations that I had slowly accumulated over the years. I knew what my gut feeling was telling me but I couldn't efficiently and fluently express myself in a way that people could understand and maybe observe themselves. Writing lets me do that. I only have a priori evidence to support what I'm trying to make known. For more credible evidence you'll be reading about a man named Buckminster Fuller. I won't go into detail about him now, but I will usually refer to him as BF or Bucky from now on. My a priori evidence is repeated observations of, and experiences with, oppressive events encountered throughout my life that I was unable to explain earlier in my youth because of a lack in my experience and vocabulary. I was also busy being "youthful."

Being preoccupied isn't a bad thing as long as it's not the politically motivated social preoccupation that prevents us from discovering the potential of our minds and abilities. Preoccupation with political control keeps distance between society and the "virtual" book of forbidden knowledge, which can be obtained through discovering your mind. I don't blame society for things being the way they are. I blame the trans – evolution of dominancy and instinct selfishness that I see in nature over into the human – created environment as control and greed. It's not our fault that things are this way, but it is our fault for not doing something about it.

For a long time, figuring out why things are the way they are was my only focus, but starting somewhere around 1994 or so, I became more interested in understanding the universe. I don't have as much time or experience with understanding the universe as I do with my social understandings, but I still have a lot of questions and statements I need to make now because of how my cosmic awareness compels me like my social awareness did. It's not in a doubting way though; it's just in a different unconventional perspective kind of way. My social experiences and observations generated doubt. I don't think I will be doubting science, just questioning it.

The gut feeling origin between my social and cosmic understandings guided me to call the second section of this book "Signals from within," meaning it is going to take awhile for what most compels me to "ascend" up from my thoughts, so to enable me to be most clear when explaining the universe as it appears to me. I have learned to question everything but to be careful how much I doubt. Questions scrutinize and generate a food source for thought and can help prove or disprove the topic at hand.

Also, asking questions shouldn't make people go on the defense. If you're going to doubt, it's a good idea to have some knowledge of what it is you doubt. And remember, the objective in any conversation should be productive dialogue and not waging a war of short sighted opinions from the egotistically confident naïve or between the jousting egos of two specialists.

Here are a couple of statements that describe how I think conversations should go.

(1) The proper projection of an opinion is an opinion that can be used and doesn't have to be deflected or ignored.

(2) The proper reception of an opinion contains ninety nine percent listening, plus one percent projected.

The projections of people's opinions are a reflection of their personality. The reason I said "are a reflection", instead of "are reflections" is because it takes more than one opinion to indicate a personality trait that you suspect a person to have. If you are going to judge, don't do it hastily, and remember, people's expectations of each other are greater than they are able to keep of themselves. We judge each other by a set of rules no one can keep. In this book, I mean to tell people how they shouldn't act, not how they should act. There is a difference.

Throughout this book I use the word "they" a lot. "They" usually means people who demonstrate or behave in the wrongfully manipulative manner I talk about in the first section of this book. I don't mean "they" in a conspiracy sense. Conspiracy is the word used by a lot of people to describe what I'm saying in this book, but I explain why the word conspiracy is not the right word in the chapter called "Obeying Nature".

If you don't want to read the whole book, then I recommend "Signals Ascend from within," "Obeying Nature," and "About Buckminster Fuller, as the chapters you should read, with the poetry, too. I also suggest that you refer to the dictionary of words that I have provided so to understand my use of a given word. What will be the historic designation of *Signals*? Information that was fortunately learned or information that was unfortunately missed due to society's present psychological state caused by subconscious preoccupation and oppression by the people we are suppose to be able to trust.

As B.F. wrote in *Critical Path*,

"Exploring, experiencing, feeling, and to the best of my ability, acting strictly and only on my Intuition I became impelled to write this book."

Signals Ascend from Within

To begin with, I have a few statements about myself that say a lot:
 My mind is my greatest ally and my greatest adversary.
 The world sucks – life is a beautiful thing but very intense for me.
 My biggest gripe is with our irresponsible stewardship of the planet and the treatment of its inhabitants, especially our own kind.
 And finally, I strongly believe that the core of human progress, social control, and many individuals' level of living is from the misuse of one's awareness or position to wrongfully manipulate others with lower awareness or position.

 These broad statements are what the "Signals Ascend from within" section of this book is about. I'll come right out and say it: I am a negative person on the surface, but what I am trying to say is very positive. It is bigger than all the negatives combined. I'm fighting for all to get what they deserve. What the world encourages I'm trying to stop, which is selfishness, dominancy, and the ego.
 What I have to say should not be ignored. People are inheritively and inherently getting smarter to the ways of the world so that oppression and suppression are widely used tools by people who misuse their knowledge to control societies. Also, "public privilege is inversely proportional to its population." The bigger the population, the less it is allowed to do.
 Staying on this course is destined for compounding problems. "Public worldly wisdom will spawn revolution."
 People won't know exactly what's going on, but they'll have a hunch that something is wrong, and it will get them thinking and acting. People are going to be very upset when they discover that not only are the methods used by higher awareness to control societies much like a donkey chasing a carrot on the end of a string, but they are a plastic carrot we are chasing. The difference between society's fishing pole and the higher awareness's fishing pole for catching a better life is that we're forced to use barbless hooks and they're not. When the rule is "catch and release," we're the only ones throwing our livelihoods back, and it's into their buckets. People aren't going to stay the same once they start to

discover this to be true.

I'm not saying we should have a total rebellion. I just want to make it known that the have, have – not scenario that describes our existence is totally unjust and un – evolved and that humanity does not deserve to go any further in its courses until fairness and respect are the main objectives of society and its leaders. I mean a legitimate "fair deal" for everybody. It's very unfair that people with lower abilities are taken advantage of by people with higher abilities, but it is also not fair when people have to give up something just because they have more. It's just a question of how did they get that "more?"

As you will read throughout "Signals Ascend from within," I want to be fair to everyone and not try not to skew it towards people who have less, even though that is what is most pronounced and is where the most wrong is being done. As I try to establish a fair playing field, however, the parameters that determine what is fair will likely take away from most that have "a lot."

The systems that rulers use to maintain control over their subjects are largely based on deceit of greedy and power hungry individuals. I think Thomas Malthus was wrong in his reasoning of why there are the haves and the have – nots. Briefly he says, "If the haves let the have – nots benefit from their abilities, it would be a degradation, or threat, to their own well – being." To me, that is the most un – evolved, selfish, and illegitimate reasoning that is still believed and practiced today. He does have a point about how the population increases faster that the food supply, but that's no reason to act as we do. "There is enough in the world for everyone's needs, but there isn't enough for everyone's greed," as Frank Buchman said.

Other people have written things about why life is so hard, why there are the haves and have – nots, and why the haves are the fittest to survive. For the ones who say it's a justified existence, I'm here to prove them wrong. They "ill" legitimately think they're number one, and they have to show it by number two – ing on everybody else, "ill" meaning to have a component of evil.

I think our leaders and providers think that, since the survival of the fittest fact of life doesn't need to be classified as moral or immoral, if it's just the way it is and you can't change it, we shouldn't feel guilty. No, we should feel guilty. It's not as unchangeable as having to eat or sleep.

I feel very passionate about trying to show people that most of us are not getting what we deserve. It is the main reason why I wrote this book, as well as to insure that my struggles do not go in vain. To be behind one's time is permanent death. To be ahead of ones' time, you're only dead temporarily, but Confucius says, "Dead is dead." It saddens me tremendously to watch most of society be misled, played, deceived, and abandoned by people we are supposed to be able to trust.

The reason the world is like this is because we still act like nature. We act this way because either we don't know it, or we can't control it, like males who have to be dominant with their girlfriends or wives, or in their interactions with others and women who are attracted to nature's dominate behaviors in males, perceiving them to be the strongest to survive. That's totally un – evolved for both men and women. Nature's dominancy should only be used to protect our survival and not how to deal with each other. To be dominant at what you're good at is an ok form of dominancy, but nature's "survival of the fittest" form of dominancy is still very much embedded in our psychologies. Society ignores nature's dominancy by naively saying, "That's the way it is, you can't change it, so go with it," and "You will benefit proportional to the level of your awareness or position in this psychological food chain scenario in which we live, where most of society is plankton." Again, this is totally un – evolved.

From my physiologically evolved, thousand years in the future, a priori interpretation of how things should be, I believe that we can only fulfill the destination of humanity as a whole, but our individual psychologies seek self – equilibrium. That is why we say, "doing what is best for me" or "looking out for number one." You do have to look out for yourself to a point, or you won't be able to play your part in the "whole," but it should not be applied in every case. Doing what is best for you is a behavior from our previously having to live in an uncertain fluctuating environment. We originated in that environment. Our not so truthful or trustworthy leaders and providers recognized this as a way to control us and to keep us divided, not psychologically united. They don't want us to unite too much, or they might end up like the grasshoppers in *It's a Bug's Life*. That's why we are taught to speak our mind with confidence and an ego.

I think true self – confidence does not include an ego or ignorance. We are taught to judge each other on how we rate, or fit in, with society, a "who are you" and "what do you have" mentality. This helps maintain their "divide to conquer and keep divided to keep conquered objective, as B.F. calls it. We should be confident when we talk but not with an ego or ignorance. We need to get rid of the team – destroying ego. The ego must be a trans – evolutionary, or secondary, behavior of dominance. It's encouraging to meet or watch people who have evolved away from nature's psychological dictation. To people who rate themselves and others by whom they are or what they have, I to say to them, "Social status and status symbols are superficial wants that show a lack in the ability to possess self – satisfaction without having to intentionally display signs of wealth or social position." Many have those possessions and titles because there is one set of rules for the masses and another set of rules for "those in the know." If everyone had to obey the same set of rules, then an absolute control system would work: not an absolute control in which everyone is unhappy, but a control that protects both the earth and its inhabitants from being pillaged. If we had certain regulations and restrictions from the start, then we wouldn't know any different. Life, though, would still get progressively better as technology and the complementary ephemeralization increased. We should periodically remind ourselves of how things were in the past to keep us in check.

There should only be two rules for living in the human environment: you're not allowed to unjustifiably take away from the earth or from other people, and, our utmost concern should be the welfare of all the children on planet earth. They're not adults yet, and they shouldn't be subjected to the expectations and punishments of a rigid, conditioned society. Children are our future. We can progress faster if we protect and promote our children's well – being. The proper upbringing of children, without nature's selfish behaviors, is crucial to sooner expedite humans' departure from earth.

The world, however, even steals candy from babies and children. Also, we say we are doing our best not to harm the earth, but I find that to be untrue. I disagree that we are doing our best not to harm the earth. On the other hand, however, I don't necessarily support the people who protect the earth. They go too far in the opposite direction. We are the animals, too. We have the right to use the earth to better our existence and comforts. The difference is that we have the choice of what animals in nature we use as our teachers or examples. We choose to be like gophers in the garden. We wrongfully exploit and abuse nature's resources. Nature should be glad we are here, not sad. By now, we should be experts in being symbiotic with the earth and its inhabitants. We should also be symbiotic with our non – biological resources because biology depends on those resources.

Big businesses are pathetic. They blame our situation on everybody. They are the smart ones who provide the things that are harming the earth and us. The main responsibility falls on them. It becomes society's problem when they don't comply with what our leaders say we need to do in order to make a long – term success of humans on earth. Our governments and providers, I feel, should be the main social parents with any adult being a support parent, but, instead, they are like parents who blame their kids for being late on their house payment. We're supposed to set good examples for our children and others for how to treat each other and the earth. It's big business and government responsibility to initiate and practice sensible behavior, and it is society's responsibility to follow suit. The industrial revolution should never have happened without recycling going hand in hand. Every discovery or invention should have been treated with respect and responsibility. Anything that harms the earth should only be used sparingly until a more "earth happy" alternative can replace it. By now, we would be a lot farther along with low to no pollution transportation and with wind and solar power for other uses.

The best interests of power and greed, however, dictate otherwise. The people with the most smarts are spending most of their time using those smarts to subliminally control and deceive us. I say again, "We should only be using earth – harming products when the benefits for all are great, and we responsibly use them." We need to promote offering big rewards for coming up with "earth happy" inventions. Look how we come up with groundbreaking technology when it is needed to win a war. That same effort should be applied always. As B.F. says in *Critical Path* "we must stop spending our energy account and spend more of our energy income. What we are doing is no different than burning our houses to stay warm at night. Chief Seattle said, "Contaminate your bed, and you will one night suffocate in your own waste". The Stanford Research Institute says, "The difference between mans' soot and nature's grime is that nature knows how to clean up after herself". And, I say, "Man's progress is at nature's expense, and nature's rehabilitation will be at the expense of man."

Technology would be more advanced today had not man, with his selfish pursuit of power, consciously oppressed civilizations, misusing his knowledge and suppressing the knowledge from what might have been brilliant minds. We need to start eliminating unnecessary dominant and selfish behaviors from our system. It is in the best interest of future generations. I want people to accept this as truth and not act incredulously. The eventual realization of the truth I have to say in this book is as certain as one will succumb to sleep.

It's ironic that a lot of the people I am sticking up for will be the ones who tell me I'm wrong, and it's just the way I choose to look at things. I don't hold anything against these people, but I do want to say to the people who are wrongfully manipulating others that there is a high probability that there will be an event, either environmental or social, that will disrupt your oppressive tactics, and the rules for order in society are going to change.

Where do you think the new "strongest to survive" groups or individuals are going to go? They're going to YOUR HOUSE! "Dictators ride to and fro upon tigers which they dare not dismount, and the tigers are getting hungry," said Winston Churchill.

You may notice I repeat some things three or four times. If a statement works in more than one topic, then I'll put it in there. I also repeat things for emphasis, such as, "It would not please me to witness a social melt down" and "Things would be miserable for the have – nots only."

Now I want to talk about the dictionary and the alphabet. The dictionary is the best physical tool that I have that's in conjunction with my non-physical tool, the mind. The dictionary reveals a synergy of individual human input. No one person could ever create and integrate words into language as is seen when studying the dictionary. It is omni – inclusive, comprehensive, and complete. Complex language that is broken down in the dictionary is good evidence that our minds may be separate from the brains.

As old as most words are in the dictionary, it shows that the cutting edge of brain/mind evolution is way ahead of what is classified as "com-

AMERICA — THE LAND OF THE FREE* ~3/31
*SOME RESTRICTIONS APPLY) PLUS SHIPPING AND HANDLING
?(your)   SEE RECEIVER FOR DETAILS
                                           SUBJECT TO CHANGE WITHOUT NOTICE

1ST ATTEMPT

OBEYING NATURE

IF YOU'VE EVER WONDERED "WHY IS LIFE SO HARD", OR "WHY DO SOME PEOPLE HAVE ALOT WHILE OTHERS HAVE NONE", AND YOU WANT TO OBTAIN SOME KIND OF UNDERSTANDING, START BY MAKING A COMPREHENSIVE COLLECTION OF OBSERVATIONS OF NATURE WITHOUT HUMANS IN THE PICTURE. INCLUDED IN THIS OBSERVAT SCRAP BOOK IS ANY PAST OBSERVATIONS AND EXPENSES THAT WERE CONSCIOUSLY OR SUBCONSCIOUSLY REMEMBERED BY THE BRAIN THAT RETRIEVES, ARRANGES, AND PRESENTS THEM TO YOU IN THOUGHT EITHER AS RANDOM OF THEIR COMPLEXES

① BB2

2ND ATTEMPT

OBEYING NATURE

LIFES INTERACTIONS, IN ALL ITS BRUTALITY AND BEAUTY. A SPECTRUM (IF YOU WILL) OF FIXED OR MIXED BEHAVIORS FOUND EITHER SINGLE OR IN GROUPS LARGE & SMALL. IT IS A SPECTRUM THATS BLACK TO WHITE ON ONE END IS THE SELFISHNESS OF BLACK, NOT LETTING ANY COLORS BE GENERATED BY ANOTHER AND THE TOTAL UNON THE OTHER END BELFISHNESS OF WHITE LIGHT THAT VIRTUALLY LETS ALL EXPERIENCE THE COLORS WITHIN, FROM MY MOSTLY A SPECTATORS EXPERIENCE I (THROUGH THOROUGH OBSERVATION)

6 • Signals

ATTEMPT #3

OBEYING NATURE

LIFES INTERACTIONS, IN BOTH ALL ITS BRUTALITY AND BEAUTY — A SPECTRUM IF YOU WILL OF FIXED OR MIXED BEHAVIORS, BOTH & PSYCHOLOGICAL RESPONSES TO THE EVER CHANGING ENVIRONMENT AND TO COSMIC CONSIDERATIONS, PAST AND PRESENT EVOLUTIONARY INCLUSIONS (THINGS MANIFESTED) IN THE PHYSICAL ACTIONS OBSERVED IN NATURE AND ALSO OBSERVED, SEPARATED IN THE UNIQUE HUMAN CREATED ENVIRONMENT. IS IT AN ANOMALY OR REALLY PERHAPS PART OF EVOLUTION THAT IN NATURE, THE SPECIES WITHIN THE NATURAL ENVIRONMENT ARE IN A CONSTANT STRUGGLE FOR SURVIVAL DUE TO THE COMPETITION FOR AND A USUALLY LACK IN THE FOOD SUPPLY.

RCOMPONENT
OR THE MOST PART

RB1

ATTEMPT #4

OBEYING NATURE

LIFES INTERACTIONS, WITH ALL ITS BRUTALITY AND BEAUTY, A SPECTRUM IF YOU WILL OF FIXED OR MIXED PHYSICAL BEHAVIORS THAT MIRROR OR REFLECT THE PSYCHOLOGICAL RESPONSES TO THE EVER CHANGING ENVIRONMENTS OF LOCAL, GLOBAL, OR COSMIC CONSIDERATIONS. THESE BEHAVIORS ARE OBSERVED IN THE FLORA AND THE FAUNA OF THEIR OWN KIND AND BETWEEN DIFFERENT SPECIES. HUMANS ORIGINATED IN THAT ENVIRONMENT, ALSO BUT HAVE SINCE EVOLVED TO A POINT WHERE WE HAVE CREATED OUR OWN ENVIRONMENT. (ARE WE AN ANOMALY OR ARE A MORE PERMANENT PART OF UNIVERSE EVOLUTION OR PROGRESSION)? *OPP

Signals • 7

mon intelligence."

Sometimes, when I look up a word, I end up looking up four or five words because that's where the initial word about which I was inquiring led me. It can turn into a journey! There sure are a lot of words that are very similar but differ only in an inclusion of an emotion or some other subtle difference. I think if something can't be described with two or three words in a compound word, then it should get its own word. We should also pronounce words as they are spelled. I think our minds would agree that we need to clean house in our Lexicon a little bit. To sum up my thoughts on our complex language and the accompanying dictionary, I perplexedly say, "Wow!"

Now I have two questions about our Alphabet. If W is supposed to be spelled with two U's, then why do most of us and all computers use two V's? If Q and U occur together most of the time, then shouldn't they be next to each other in the Alphabet? The Alphabet would then be – Q, U, R, S, T, V, double – V (W), X, Y, Z. If you find this to be unusual, wait till you see an evolution of how I write. It's very unconventional – see figures 1 – 4.

My writing is that way because it evolves as I write it down. I have to keep re – writing my thoughts until I get to what it is I'm trying to say. It might be looked at as inadequate, but to me it shows the individuality and diversity of people and that I don't let my limitations stop me, and you shouldn't either. Another limitation I have, at this time, is that I can't fluently choose the right words and put those words into sentences when having dialogue. In other words, I have a hard time turning my thought waves into sounds waves. I have a nitro methane powered mind using a gasoline powered brain.

A common goal of all should be that of increasing our knowledge and understanding. Being different in doing, that is a good thing. It shows you are following your own way of expressing yourself and not the ways of conditioned society's rigid expectations of how you should express yourself. "If a man does not keep pace with his companions, perhaps it is because he hears a different drummer. Let him step to the music which he hears, however measured or far away," Henry David Thoreau wrote in *Walden*. For me, it's not one set path, but many paths that I take when presenting my findings or opinions.

I wonder if the mind is just using the brain as a stepping – stone in its own evolution. Bucky separates the brain and mind by describing the brain as the sorter – retriever – arranger. It sorts through, arranges, and compares images of the past or of events happening right now.

Bucky describes mind as having the ability to recognize generalized principals, such as how tension always accompanies compression, convex and concave, or mass attraction and precession. Mind also recognizes, not through repetition, things that have not happened yet. Mind recognizes what is important and programs the brain. Our brains are unique, but it is the barely tapped capabilities of mind that is the next step in our evolution.

Sometimes I put the word "the" in front of the word "mind," and sometimes I don't. I do that to show that I think maybe the mind is a separate entity and not accredited to the human brain.

Some people think that humans are the final product in the sequence of biological evolution, but I think that goes in line with thinking that the earth is at the center of the universe. Right now, we are thinking we will be taking our bodies with us when we leave earth for good. It's egotistical to think we can take our bodies into space any farther than our own solar system. Space travel is a mind connected to body existence, and that to me is a brain – oriented and reasoned direction, egotistical in a way. An ego is an adverse side of intelligence.

There is so much more I want to say in this book, but it's never ending. I can always come up with a more complete and inclusive way to describe what compels me, but I am satisfied with what I have, and I want to share with others my thoughts.

I hope this book will trigger people to realize and explore their own minds. There is so much we don't know, and we need all the input we can get.

Isaac Newton said, "I don't know what I may appear to the world, but to myself, I seem to have been only like a boy playing on the sea shore and diverting myself in now and then finding a smoother pebble, or a prettier shell, than the ordinary, whilst the great ocean of truth lay all undiscovered before me." Accomplishing change that's necessary for our continuance could be easy if selfishness and dominancy vanished, but, realistically, it can be achieved over time through our actions and words toward our children and each other. I am very positive when I look at my objectives, but I'm negative when I describe what bothers me and what I feel needs to be fixed. I have positive message with a negative projection.

I want to live way out in the forest so I can enjoy my life the way I feel I deserve. I have enough experiences and observations of the world to keep me busy thinking and writing for a while. I can use action at a distance, through words, to try to help people. I will always try to help people break free of their limitations. I need to go to the forest so I can continue that because I am on the brink of cerebral meltdown. If you like what I say in this book, and you want to hear more, hope that I get there soon.

I would be farther along if I didn't make mistakes. I've made some big ones, but, to date, I've involuntary donated approximately $200,000 dollars to capitalism because of the exploitation of the third world labor resource. I want the less fortunate to have a better life. Everyone should be able to live wherever they want. Capitalism, however, is forcing me to compete with people who are use to living under bushes and eating lizards. If they're qualified to do the job then they should get the wage that was established before they got here. It also should be that the best person wins, not, that the hungriest person or most desperate person wins. Our leaders purposely allowed an influx of third – world workers to drive down wages in the United States. I don't want to participate in these practices in order to be successful. Being that this is obviously the way things are has made me want to change my fight for social success into a fight for survival. Those two things don't go together in my world.

Nature is an environment that I like to be in that helps me travel through the thought experiments I derive when diving into the philosophical abyss. It's also a good backdrop for mind release.

I also want to be in nature because I have a hard time accepting what people accept as just the way it is. I think higher awareness is purposely keeping us in the crumb – catcher, scavenger mode by asserting its dominance via structured oppression. All of this is slowly deteriorating my health and sanity. Being in nature would slow it down considerably, but I would still be thinking about the un – justs of the world. This is because of how passionate my feelings are toward what is wrongfully and manipulatively presented to us as the truth. It's totally my fault for letting things get to me. I need to address what bothers me, but I shouldn't dress in it. When I try to talk to people about it, I sometimes get drowned out by the myopic tsunami and the undertows of ignorance. It is a conditioned response, and I don't blame society for being that way, it just seems so standard and programmed. "Dare to tell the truth as you see it, and you will find yourself in trouble. It is better to learn the story everyone tells and stick with that", says B.F. in *Intuition*.

I have a poster of Albert Einstein that has a statement on it that I suspect is from someone else who found it befitting to him. It says, "Great spirits have always encountered violent opposition from mediocre minds." Sounds egotistical, but it is true. I see society as conditioned, non – thinking, and rigid. I believe it is that way because it doesn't have time to think about anything but what is relevant to the everyday existence of its individuals. They are unknowingly being manipulated by preoccupation. This makes them respond by using dialogue from what I call "The Rigida Stone," meaning a rigid, "carved in granite," response. Don't be different or make mistakes because you'll likely be persecuted. It is anti – individualism to think or act from "The Rigida Stone." I am not saying that I don't sometimes act that way, but I know I shouldn't, and I want society to stop it. I don't use the "that's the way it is, you can't change it, so get over it" excuse. I try to recognize what I am doing, and then I try to correct it. I don't exclude myself from most of my quotations, but I have considerably evolved away from most of what I call "un – evolved behavior." It is a reflex society needs to work on controlling. Something we should have abolished, we've polished. We have shown an evolution of un – evolved behaviors.

We need to quit being so eager to quote from the Rigida Stone the saying, "It's happening to you; therefore, it's your fault." It is more someone's fault for wrongfully taking advantage of others than it is that person's fault for letting someone take advantage of them. You shouldn't have to be a car salesman when buying a car or a mechanic when getting that car fixed. You shouldn't have to be a real estate agent or a geologist when buying a house or land. An average intelligence should be established as a standard to determine whether you're being taken advantage of or if you are just an idiot. Being an idiot doesn't mean it's ok for others to take advantage of you.

I agree that everyone is born a genius. It's just a matter of finding out what they are good at. Our leaders don't give us the time to find out what that genius is. We are too busy dealing with everyday "life," which they purposely complicate in order to preoccupy us and to keep us from looking this way or that way. There should not be "The Book of Forbidden Knowledge." Though it is not an actual book, that's just what it's called. There should be a generalization or synoptic wisdom class starting at kindergarten, even though students wouldn't understand it. Everyone should be educated in "The Book of Forbidden Knowledge." It is what's best for humanity as a whole.

To keep things from getting out of hand, people's innate limitations would keep too many people from achieving large – scale success. Regulations and restrictions would also prevent any potential problems. We should promote success and not worry about too many people having synoptic and synergetic awareness. My system for obtaining money in the next chapter would also help in keeping things from getting out of hand. We are severing a vital source of information by withholding knowledge, making it too hard to understand or too hard to find. They are withholding information of which they have no right depriving us. Our system is totally skewed toward the benefit of "those in the know." They are like a squirrel that drives all the other squirrels away from the food even though humans threw the food out for all of them. It is not right for people to horde knowledge.

In a legitimate existence, social, wrongful manipulation would be kept in check by all social parents. In reality, however, "the suits are in cahoots," and I am their psychological nemesis. Even if it turns out that I am wrong in my explanations of the way things are, it has the consequences that it does, the deprivation of others, and there is no legitimate reason for that behavior existing in the separate environment we have created for ourselves. We accept the way things are in our understanding of why life is so hard, however, and why there are the haves and have – nots. I'm here to get the ball of change rolling faster. We don't have to let the selfish "haves" in our back doors, or should I say, "up our back doors."

I have watched and read a lot on self help. Something I've noticed is we're taught not to change the way things are, but to change ourselves. I've been told that the problem is me, and that it is the way I look at things, but I think that is wrong. "A" problem is letting what I see bother me, and I take full responsibility for letting things bother me. "The" problem is what bothers me. Most people who don't let things bother them aren't doing a damn thing about it. If you want to be happy ignore it, if you want to be really happy then deny it even exists. To all the inside – the – box, rigid, myopic, bubble – thinkers this doesn't mean you have to be mad all the time, like I am, in order to be doing something about it. I have learned that I care too much. I choose to take notice and try to make changes. Part of my happiness depends on other people being happy, too. Oppression is a main cause of people's unhappiness, and it is also the cause of many other social problems. Writing *Signals* has been a way for me to deal with my problems, and I hope that it will help others obtain happiness and understanding.

Earning and Deserving Money

These next few pages generally layout some guidelines for earning and deserving money. This is simple in concept but it inevitably will have complications. I want to let it be known now that I know what I have to say here is a "virtual" impossibility. It is only unachievable due to selfishness and the conditioning of social understanding of the way things are to the point at which they accept that things are just the way they are, and you can't change them. The way I see it, is however, that "the intellectual's blanket of obscurity that is thrown over us as unchangeable reality is seamed by the limiting boundaries of our own synoptic wisdom that forces us to rely on those worn paths of the intellectual's explanations of so called reality to be actual reality." The reason our government lets us be pillaged is because it gets its cut, and it also eats up our available income. A legitimate system of obtaining your possessions could happen now, but the selfish survival instincts of our evolutionary past are still very much in the driver's seat. So, maybe these guidelines, these logical, fair guidelines, are for next time around, or the next time around…

My a priori, which eventually will be aposteriori, concept of a "fair payroll" goes as follows.

What is the job or task being performed? What are the risks, dangers, stresses, and strains both physically and mentally? What are the responsibilities as far as human lives, the dependency on the self or others, or the well – being of the company? What is the necessity of the job or task, and how many people are able to do the job? Did you make a significant contribution? Other considerations to determine how much you should be paid are how long have you been doing this task? How much schooling is required to qualify for the job? What are your performance abilities, reliability, and your track record? These guidelines should apply to everyone involved in a particular society or teamwork system. People who truly deserve a lot of money are still compensated through these fair and logical guidelines. I don't want to take away from someone who is rightfully deserved.

In my opinion, some jobs that don't deserve "a lot" of money are, just to name a few, athlete, actor, entertainer, talk show host, lawyer, manufacturer, marketer and sales representative, real estate agent, home loans associate, banker, etc., and basically the whole computer industry. The people who deserve a significant amount of money in the computer field are the ones who make very big contributions to its existence. The people or person who recognized and developed the properties of silicon is just one example. The people who make the contributions are usually not adequately compensated, but the ones in manufacturing and marketing do. We praise and pay them as if they made the contributions all by themselves. We should realize that, more than likely, we're compensating the wrong people and that there are uncompensated people in the discovery or development of a given advancement. When we give credit to a person for a contribution instead of saying so – and – so discovered or invented a contribution, we should say so – and – so, with his or her influences and contributors, discovered or invented a given contribution. Even with the special theory of relativity, I hear Einstein didn't have any contributors, but I think he definitely had influences. All the people before him that contributed to the pool of knowledge as a whole were his influences.

As far as people and their money go, there are some people who have a lot of money that think they deserve it because they were once poor. It's encouraging to hear rags to riches stories, but a lot of those stories are in industries that don't deserve to be rich in the first place. There is an element of struggle for their success, so I won't harp on them.

As for athletes and actors, virtually speaking, I think those so – called jobs should be done after work. To think that any of these jobs I listed deserves the money it can bring in is as unintelligent as is buying fish and chickens bone in, but at bone out prices. There was a name for people like that in earlier times. They were called "village idiots." Going to a movie or sports event does play a much needed role in society as relaxation and recreation, but, come on, people, they didn't save the world.

I have a facetious acronym for F.A.N.S.: Foolish and Naïve Spectators. It's just a joke, ok? Crowd participation, dedication, and support are all good things, don't get me wrong. It's good to break free from thinking about everyday existing once in a while. Things could still be the same in sports and entertainment or the world for a broader scope, just minus the bazillion wasted dollars on everything connected to whatever it is we like or need. There is trillions of undeserved dollars made from capitalism and other "ill" legitimate ways, and I think a significant part of that money should go to children, the handicapped and the elderly. Not making this change is an indication of the intelligence level of society as a whole. I would be embarrassed to have to tell someone from another world how our system works.

An example of how someone can make a good sum of money with an occupation that normally shouldn't pay a lot, for example, in the music industry, is by giving rewards for repeated accomplishments like, number one songs or records, remaining number one for an extended period of time, and doing that time and time again. These people helped shape our culture. There is room then for musicians like The Rolling Stones, The Beatles, The Eagles, the Elton John's, and many others in all types of music to still be adequately and justifiably compensated.

I've been told that I am jealous of people who make a lot of money. Yeah, I guess it's just me, huh? I chose the not – so – important job of roofing. I should have chosen one of those more important tasks of maintaining and progressing our existence like acting, or athletics. What was I thinking? How unrealistic of me. When will I think logically? I won't say the statement that belongs here. You can find it in the chapter "Other Statements." It's the one about logic and reasoning, but to say it in a different way now:

"Although the number of corrupt businessmen and the way they do business has changed, the intelligence of their markets has stayed the same."

To show that I am not jealous, I wouldn't attack an actor or athlete personally with my opinions because they are just the lucky recipients of people being idiots with their money. I wouldn't attack any spokes person for things like weight – loss, car manufacturers, or phone service because they are just marionette hype – emissaries for deceivers. It's the whole industry that I have a problem with so why should I take it out on an individual when it's our whole system. Remember, these guidelines for making your money are applicable to all jobs. It's not as rigid as it can imply. I believe it is fair and reasonable.

The people with whom I have the biggest problem in society are the people who misuse their awareness or position. It can be anybody. Our responsibility is proportional to the level we misuse our tools to achieve ridiculous, unjustified levels of personal living. People who deserve a lot of money are those who make significant contributions to their society or all societies. Repeated small contributions count, too, but they are less likely to be noticed. Big businesses take the credit for a contribution and exploit it for power and money. Again, I think the credits and rewards are likely going to the wrong people. The have, have – not situation is totally unjust. There isn't a "just to all" social system in which there are no have – nots, but this system we have now has got to go.

Even the ideas I have would contain haves and have – nots. People with better abilities should get more just so long it is justified and legitimate. Even if everyone made the same amount of money, there would still be the haves and the have – nots due to each person's ability to spend or save money. Always keep in mind that these ideas are from someone who wants to play fair and give participators what is due to them. To contradict myself, however, if they let people totally benefit from their abilities, they would more than likely destroy themselves, so standardized laws to control this would have to be put into place. All that needs to happen initially is a justification of earnings and possessions, if you know what I mean. I can't and won't see how or why that would or should upset the system, but it would, wouldn't it?

We have the power to take back the legitimate level of control we should have in our system, DON"T WE? The money thing kind of illuminates a lot of undeserved levels of living, DOSEN'T IT? Let's change it!

I know my system needs work, but with other logically thinking, level headed, psychologically evolved, non – politically motivated, which means no hidden agenda, realistic – thinking people, it can be a good system sometime in the future. Money does have uses other than to control us and deplete our excesses. It does make things easier, no matter what form we use. It is evident that we will be paper money free eventually. Whatever is best for the earth and what's best for us, but that won't be why they do it. Overall, money opened the ultimate window of wrongful manipulation, directly proven between the values at its origin and today. In the United States, the system that very much fulfills the best interests of political or other hidden agendas, which are being carried out on a tilted playing field, is capitalism, or should I say "crap – on – all – ism." Robbing someone with your intelligence or position, to me, is no different than robbing them with physical force. If it's survival of the fittest, then it should be survival of the fittest one hundred percent. If you're going to rob someone with intelligence, then you had better be able to conquer them physically as well. It's nature surviving, isn't it? Isn't it wrong that it is always illegal to rob someone with physical force and not always with intelligence?

I think the vast majority of businesses are Enron – structured. Enron just went too far and got caught.

Carl Sagan, the astronomer, said in the original release of *Cosmos* "The unrestrained pursuit of profit poses serious threats to the soul of our nation". My statement is that people who use human sacrifices to replace the missing rungs in their ladder of success don't deserve their success. They should have most everything taken away from them and forced to start over. I think that the way most people in businesses are doing business these days is they've just started to get the hang of the old idea of capitalism. Get everything done as cheap as you can and keep all the money: maximum profit, with zero liability. It's an intellectual food chain hierarchy system, and it's wrong. I hold governments and the intellectual power structures behind the governments responsible for being masters of wrongfully manipulating our vulnerabilities. Like our emotions, awareness's, desires, dependencies, abilities, desperations, beliefs, curiosities, available income, and most of all, our trust in them to lead us honestly and fairly which they don't. They are liars, they are cheaters, they are deceivers. They are predators and parasites on our efforts to make better lives for ourselves. They mislead, play, deceive, and abandon. They are fighting for the wishbone of the social carcass.

An example of how they do this is that they mislead us by making it look like it's not. Misleading us they use distortion, exaggeration, and stretch – the – truth sales tactics. A way they deceive us is by filling their contracts with needless complication and confusing terminology. And, if or when things go bad, they abandon ship and hide behind laws that are made by and for the people who are best at misusing their awareness or position. Such is the reason for the inflation of our wants and needs, corporate downsizing, or a third world labor source. Bucky says all of this with two words "comprehensive deprivation." He also says, "It's survival only of the fittest selfishness." Inflation is an oppressive counter – action to social ephemeralization. Ephemeralization is a B.F. word that describes how humans are progressively doing more with less, less time, energy, and materials. What once took seventy two thousand tons of oceanic cable is now being out – performed by a five hundred pound satellite. We are doing more with less in the mining, refining, manufacturing, cultivating, transportation, and distribution of our goods and resources.

Ephemeralization should be a benefit to all involved in the teamwork system in which the ephemeralization takes place. The fact that this is not the case is a major downfall and will be what spawns a rebellion that could end in the collapse of the world as we know it. It doesn't have to be this way, but at least future generations will have a better chance at getting a fair deal. Society is slowly becoming aware that this is true, and it may be too late to fix. It should have been dealt with a long time ago. "Public worldly wisdom will spawn revolution." It must be done for future generations.

The Enlightenment and the industrial revolution would have been good opportunities to show that we don't have to act like nature in order to reach a personal equilibrium, but we failed to do so. Our behaving like nature should have started to leave us shortly after the arrival of a comprehensive mind. We are still a long ways away from separating ourselves from our psychologically less evolved, act on instinct, brain – only ancestors. How do I know that we have a long way to go? Well, at the present time we are putting on the walls of museums the pictures of the people who are best at acting like un – psychologically evolved nature. They mistakenly represent to us good, smart business, and we can learn from them how to be successful, how to be the "fittest" to survive. To me, most, but definitely not all, of the people we praise should be stopped and discredited. If they are dead, they should be dug up, denied a grave, and discredited.

We also have a long way to go because we are promoting crap – on – all – ism in other countries, presenting it as a good system for all. I want to run through the streets in other countries where capitalism is being promoted and yell out, "The selfish are coming, the selfish are coming." The way capitalism has turned out in America is described by Gerald Piel as "waking from the American dream to realize it was a dream few Americans live in their waking hours."

"America, the land of the free, plus shipping and handling, some restrictions apply, see deceiver for details, subject to change without notice, results are typical." Pretty harsh isn't it? Be careful not to exaggerate what I am saying. I'm sure I've offended enough people already. I really mean corporate America, or just "business" America. I strongly support our troops. We are the freest country in the world. People can unite, but it takes a crisis to do so. My support stops at the abuse of others and the earth. I think people would agree that this is common practice in America and that true Americans should not support this kind of behavior. In any country, it's all caused by the politics of power and greed. Politics do more to damage to the well – being and success of humans than an ego does to team efforts.

I'm not saying I want to live anywhere else other than way out in the forest where my stress would be different but reduced.

I know that the changes I would like to see happen can't be initiated in any power structured system in the world today. Psychological evolution is the avenue through which these kinds of changes can manifest. I know I am at least planting some evolutionary spores that will germinate when they land in the right conditions, which is an inquisitive unconditioned mind.

Well, I knew this topic was going to be mostly about people who don't deserve their money. I tried to be more positive, but it's a deferred positive. I am trying to initiate a system that is fair for all. I want to make people aware that a lot of us aren't getting what we deserve. I know I'm negative, but should I deny reality for the sake of not sounding negative? What enrages me is that their parasitic prosperity isn't limited to adults who are wrongfully classified as being in the "you should have known" category. No, they have to mess with our children's education and other child orientated programs. Children don't even know what's going on. Why can't we see what's going on? **The abuse of our children should be what triggers us to make changes.** I think the way our leaders control us is very much the same as adults deal with children. I don't mean like babies but in the way parents can anticipate and predict child behaviors before they start acting in a particular way. They can appease, divert, or stop them before they get out of hand. Our leaders do the same thing with society.

Big businesses say they care, but, "You can't see misery on people you can't see," said (unknown).

I feel we should confront the negative so we can enjoy some positive, a realistic positive and not an "ignorance is bliss" form of positive or happiness. Happiness is the goal, but ignorance, or to ignore, doesn't change what needs to be changed. Actually it seals our fate.

Not everyone needs to be involved in these changes, but they should be aware that there are people out there who will make sure they are not being taken advantage of. I am aware that there are people watching out already. I am on their side. "Most are only cutting away at the branches. Not many of us are hacking away at the roots," said Henry David Thoreau in *Walden*. Change needs to happen to legitimize human accomplishment and to earn the right to proceed in fulfilling our purpose in "our" universe.

From the Womb to the Tomb

I departed my sheltered genesis to greet a breech arrival with the choking umbilical chord of society that's dangling me over life's struggling ledges of bottomless suffering and forced conformity, and will get quickly severed upon the exhaustion of my pre – determined, conscious/sub – conscious, involuntary, sacrificial contributions to deficiencies in the courses of this selfish intellectual domination.

Rage and the Bay of Wisdom

As I search for the reasons for this blood on my hands and this glass at my feet that I created from shattering the raging windows of anger, I found windows that can be broken by anger but only by knowledge. As I break these windows, I still find glass at my feet but there is no blood on my hands.

After holding some shards of knowledge, I can now see why there is no blood on my hands. And, if there was blood, it would not be my blood of life but the blood of other people's lives, caused by and combined with the blood of my moral heart, which can get pierced by misusing the shards of power acquired when shattering the windows of knowledge.

I choose to have my own blood of life on my hands but with an understanding that the reason the blood is there is because of the injustice of the world, and also, knowing that if I unregrettably spill any blood from my moral heart, I won't be able to live happily ever after my life.

Obeying Nature

Life's interactions, with all their brutality and beauty, are a spectrum, if you will, of fixed or mixed physical behaviors that mirror or reflect the psychological responses to the ever – changing environments of local, global, and cosmic considerations. These behaviors are observed in the interactions of the fauna of different species and between the same species. These behaviors are also seen in the flora, too, but not in a psychological sense.

Humans originated in this environment but have since evolved to a point where they have created their own environment inside of their original environment. Are we an anomaly, or are we a more permanent part of universal evolution or progression? I say evolution or progression because I think that evolution and progression are two different things. What I interpret by looking in the dictionary is that these two words are closer together than I feel they should be. I want to put some distance between the two words.

It is evolution when a system does something different than that type of system normally does in the progressive sequence of that system's existence. Eventually, if it's an evolution, all or most of the same systems would have this new change, whether for the better or for the worst of that system type. A permanent propagated mutation is evolution whereas just a mutation is an abnormality in that individual systems DNA sequence. A mutation, however, could also be considered to be an evolutionary attempt or maybe a survival security measure where a species generates precautionary mutations to cover the possibility of an unexpected large change in its environment.

Systems "progress" through their existence pretty much the same as other systems of their kind. An evolution is a permanent change in a usually "the – same – sequence progression." So, instead of saying, "as the sun evolves," we should say; "As the sun progresses". If we see that suns now do something different that they usually do in their normal progression of a sun's existence, and it's not classified as a short – term mutation or event, then we could "possibly" document it as an evolutionary event in the life cycle of suns as a whole, or at least in the system in which they are involved. Just as a thought, scientists use many different aspects when creating an evolutionary sequence of faunal succession. What would that sequence look like if we used only visual clues as our guide to create a picture of our evolutionary trail?

Getting back to the physical manifestations of psychological responses to a constantly changing environment. When I observe nature, without including humans, I observe that the species within are, for the most part, in a constant struggle for survival due to a usual lack in the food supply, along with a competition for living and breeding sites that fluctuate according to local, global, or cosmic effects imposed in long or short – term, environment – altering, and oscillating events. These fluctuations in the environment result in Darwin's natural selection, the regulation of all species through a species / environment confrontation, an "adapt or die out" situation.

Also in these frequent times of shortage, a survival of the fittest between the same species and between different species exists and takes aim at the so – called weak. I say the so – called weak because being the fittest to survive can be accomplished three ways: legitimately, not – legitimately, and "ill" – legitimately.

Legitimate survival is where strength is demonstrated without involuntary or unknown contributions from the same species or other species that are also trying to be the fittest to survive. When you are the food is the only exception is this. Legitimacy can be found at the justified existence end of the behavioral spectrum.

In a not – legitimate existence, strength is acquired through taking advantage of others' despair before it is ok to do so. Acquisition of any remaining food supply or shelter should happen at the time of death or abandonment by the species that occupies that space. It would be a justified incident of the strong surviving because of the weak, and that's ok just so long the acquirement isn't premature. Not – legitimate survival has its gray area with legitimate survival and "ill" – legitimate survival. Non – legitimate survival is the middle part of the behavioral spectrum.

An "ill" – legitimate existence, unfortunately, is the most common behavior in nature's environment and in the human environment. The two environments are separate, which I'll explain in a minute, but first I describe an "ill" – legitimate existence as the deliberate interference or the intentional cause of failure by destruction or robbery of another species' efforts to be the fittest to survive.

"Ill" means having a component of evil, selfishness, and deception, the dark end of the behavioral spectrum, with legitimacy at the other end and everything inbetween.

The difference between nature acting "ill" – legitimately and humans acting the same way is that humans have a choice of what behaviors should be ok and which ones aren't, nature doesn't. Nature behaving "ill" – legitimately is nature's flaw. The truly strong in nature and in the human environment should be able to survive without "ill" – legitimate behaviors. A species should be able to survive as if it were the only one of its kind on earth, and there were no other species from which to steal food or shelter. It's just you against Mother Nature, and trying not to be some other species' lunch. Like I said earlier, being the food is the only time when involuntary contribution is acceptable. I don't like it, but it is legitimately a strong surviving over the weak scenario.

The dominant species in nature, not including humans, and dominant humans in the environment we have created for ourselves depend on others for their existence in ways that shouldn't credit that species as being the strongest to survive. I wonder if, when mass extinctions occur, the ones acting legitimately would be the ones found still alive because they didn't depend on theft or deceit of others to stay alive.

Non – ethically speaking, people who can't make it in nature would be taken care of by nature, and it would be proportional to their lack of their ability to survive. We don't have to leave people out in the cold, however, due to the tremendous advantages of the unique human environment. Instead of showing compassion and virtually ending despair for members of our species, they either make them fail sooner, or they prolong their despair for personal gain. I am not saying that they should make up what everyone else is lacking, but they shouldn't make it worse. That is exactly what they do, however, they make it worse. The people who make it worse are the parasitic, wrongfully manipulative, "ill" – legitimate big businesses or other sub – parasitic non – deserving groups or individuals.

I know, without a doubt, that existing legitimately is very possible because I can observe that in nature and in our own environment. It's hard to find, but it's there. Legitimate behavior occupies a small part of the behavior spectrum but will become more common as we evolve psychologically. I think the species in nature's environment will always be a reflection of that environment, but I think, as earth reaches its own equilibrium, nature will have regressed out of the picture. Humans can almost psychologically equilibrate despite earth's non – equilibrium, but the whole universe would have to be in equilibrium in order for humans to be in total psychological equilibrium because I think that we, too, psychologically reflect the physical behaviors of systems of which we are comprised or in which we are involved.

I ask myself why humans behave the way they do and realized that, being animals ourselves, we originated in but separated ourselves through the brain and mind complementary from the rest of the animal kingdom. Our existence and possessions, though, should be subject to validation of the legitimacy of that existence. Unfortunately and unnecessarily, the instinctive reactions and behaviors caused by the cyclic or random shortages that occur in nature have trans – evolved over into the human environment as a new name for selfishness. That name is greed. We should have left "ill" – legitimate and not – legitimate behaviors behind in our transition over into our clearly separate, technologically advanced, electrical, mechanical, and materially enhanced human environment. Instead, something we should have abolished, we've polished.

I say that because, in nature, the animals in that environment are governed by unconscious instinctive acts, a "brain only" mode. In the human environment that was created through our unique brain – mind complementary, however, those behaviors are conscious deliberate acts, and I find that to be unacceptable behavior. We can only fulfill the destination of humanity as a whole, but our individual psychologies seek self – equilibrium. That's why there are the sayings, "looking out for number one", and, "doing what is best for me." You do have to look out for yourself to a point, or you won't be able to participate in the "whole", but doing what's best for you should not be what is done in every case.

An ability we have is to realize that life's requirements can be obtained without involuntary contributions from other people. It's true that there isn't enough to go around if all were to waste our resources like the present practices by those at the top of this "ill" – legitimate psychological food chain, where most of society is plankton. It is true that the population increases faster than the food supply, but that is the doom of nature outside of the brain – mind co – existent, life – enhancing, and insuring, accomplishments of humans. I can see that the population is one thing we can't control even if the economy takes a total dive. Our life propagation instincts are as hard to change as our dominant or selfish instincts.

Population issues are something we should have as a top priority. I know that they are important issues, but that is not what this book is about. I will ask the question, though: could a reason why we are oppressed and stressed be that the high in the psychological food chain subliminal dictators are making an attempt to regulate the population by making our minds and bodies less life productive? I know that the method of protecting their best interests goes way deeper than I can comprehend. It's a "guild" that gives a "gelded" explanation, and they do it with no guilt.

The information they give us is in "formation." And it's in a formation that keeps us blind to the integrated truth. The fact that we came from nature doesn't justify our actions of illegitimate behavior. We must exist legitimately or not at all.

To exist most efficiently, we should have an intellectual hierarchy because it is beneficial to have the most competent person at each task needing to be done in sustaining and improving our levels of existence, but there should not be a psychological food chain. The limiting abilities of your own psychology and any physical considerations should not be accompanied by a price to be paid to any or all that are above you in awareness or position.

I still say that people with better abilities should be paid more according to the chapter, "Earning and Deserving Money." It's not our fault that nature taught us the selfish way, but it is our fault for not doing something about it. There are times, though, when the saying, "what might not be good for some is good for the whole," should be applied in certain infrequent circumstances. No one person or group of people, however, should be in constant contribution, as are societies or any of its subdivisions, to the parasitic capitalist's selfish dominancy and money driven objectives. The higher you are in awareness, the more responsibility you carry for participating in these behaviors.

Most people are just doing what they are taught and what they observe. Acting in this manner with comprehension and calculated deception is truly "ill" – legitimate. To those who practice these behaviors with comprehension, may your feces come out in shards. You've had plenty of time to evolve.

To show that I'm not blindly attacking the way things are, listen to what I have to say about the conspiracy theory. It seems to be a popular word for describing the way things are, but, if we say it's a conspiracy for humans, then I would have to say that the other animals are conspiring against each other also. We've been using an inter – species food chain system that was already in place before we arrived in the picture. If you don't obey nature, how can you survive? How can you change something that's been in place since the beginning? Nature does it unconsciously. Humans do it consciously. Conspiring, then, is a different word for "acting like nature," It's not isolated to humans.

We are supposed to be evolved, but instead, we are conditioned to say, "That's the way it is and you can't change it," Of course, we can change it. It would be nice if the transition went smoothly, but it probably won't catch on for a few more social control meltdowns.

There's a song by Joe Satriani on his CD, *Flying in a Blue Dream*, called "I Believe,". There are some good lyrics in it. Here is the chorus:

I believe we can change anything.
I believe we can rise above it.
I believe there's a reason for everything.
I believe in my dreams.

Adults are a product of their environment just like kids are. We believe and act as we experience and as we are taught. These behaviors are mostly anti – human progress and anti – unity behaviors that are encouraged behaviors to keep us separated to a certain degree and maintain a large percentage of us in crumb – catcher scavenger mode.

I think the upper class considers societies to be composed of the "pee – poles" (people), the "cum – sumers" to their dominant, selfishly directed psychologies. Those behaviors should only be in our past and not in the present due to the unique development of our brains and the inclusion of the possible separate entity, "mind," I separate mind from brain, though not like B.F. does, because, as I mentioned earlier, maybe humans are just the best vessel for the mind in its own evolution, or just in exist at all. Mind may well be separate from the brain. Mind has really shown its potential in the past one hundred or so years, manifested in material objects and technology. These tremendous advancements are hard to justify using a brain only, accrediting to human advancement.

All the time before the explosion of mind's physical manifestations, mind was gathering information and making tools so it could spread its wings and fly. This all took time, but it has made our lives so much better and has enabled us to embrace our clearly separate, fortunate awakenings to the treasures of the earth and universe. Mind also allows us to ponder why we are here. Invention is mind. Abstract is mind. All of human accomplishment or ponderings are exercises for mind development and evolution.

I have a tape called *The Creation of the Universe*. A sentence that jumps out at me is "Maybe life is just a phase in the on – going dance of energy." That statement sounds very plausible, but what I always want to mention about statements on topics like this is that, whether it be my work or somebody else's, I don't carve anything in granite. I don't think any theory is exactly right. This explanation about life is a good example of a comprehensive imagination, and it is a very good example of showing that the brain and the mind are likely separate. I think people deny this because it is sounds mystical.

I don't like to use words or descriptions that people associate as "freaky" thought. Metaphysical is one of those words, but it is the proper word for what it describes. It describes mind, and that's not freaky. It's just not a commonly known or possessed entity. When Einstein conceived his theory of relativity by saying," What would it look like if you could catch up to a light wave," that was purely metaphysical. It can also be called an intuitive imagination, which is a product of mind. Mind is our final frontier and may be eternal the brain is not.

Bucky showed me his ideas of the differences between brain and mind in his book *Intuition*. I knew the two were different, but he explains it very nicely. It's very deep, but basically he says the brain is the computer, and mind is the programmer.

In *Intuition*, B.F. talks about whether or not humans have a special role in the universe or if we are just observers or spectators. He suggests that humans, because of mind, do have a greater role in universal evolution other than constructor – destructor. *Intuition* is very difficult reading, much like all of Bucky's stuff. I wrote some suggestions on how to absorb his work in the chapter devoted just to him called, "About Buckminster Fuller."

Mostly, I read that he attributes mind to humans. I don't, but I haven't read all his work, and a lot of it leaves me in the dust.

My intuition tells me that humans and the mind are indeed separate. That mind has its own destination, and humans are just the best vessel. Mind is operating through us and is us. The body could be just a stepping – stone of mind evolution. I don't want mind to be associated with precognition. I've read and watched a lot of things, and I don't want to take credit for something I may have subconsciously recorded in my head from somewhere else. I keep a watch out for it, but it is possible to have two or more people come up with the same idea without knowledge of each other's work.

Getting back to what this topic is about, which is "Obeying Nature," I want to point out that we really haven't evolved as much as we claim we have. Humans started to evolve more rapidly when we started to eat meat and when our evolutionary advancements, like tool – making and agriculture, gave us a lot more time to think about other things other than existing from day to day, a "what will I eat" and "where will I sleep" preoccupation of our inner, undiscovered, unpursued curiosities and intuitions.

Today, preoccupation is a tool used by "those in the know" to keep us from psychologically evolving too quickly and possibly discovering their deliberate, "calculated use" of psychologically un – evolved behaviors. In order for our existence to be legitimate, we must start eliminating the "ill" – legitimate behaviors of our origins, which should have happened a long time ago. Nature will more than likely always be nature because it is more "affected" by the "effects" of an uncertain environment than we are, for now anyway. We need to realize that life and the world are two different things even though they are widely interpreted as being the same. I don't see the two as being the same, and here is why.

When something happens in the human environment that isn't fair, we say, "Life isn't fair," and we promptly and myopically respond with the "It's happening to you, therefore, it's your fault" mentally.

To me, however, there is life, and then there's the world. Life has unfairness to it because you don't know what the cosmos is going to send you in life through your own genetic inner workings or by happenstance of wrong place, wrong time events that happen outside one's self. The reason the world isn't fair is because people at the top of the psychological food chain purposely make it that way, wrongfully thinking that they have to obey nature's dictation, or extinction would be certain. In reality, natures inter and inner – species survival behaviors are an unwelcome evolutionary passenger in human psychology that severely disrupts, what little there is of, our evolution toward peace and fairness. A lot of what we call life not being fair is due to un – evolved world inflictions.

We humans do not deserve to go any farther in pursuing our destination until we can legitimately exist. Only then should we be able to continue toward satisfying our curiosities and understandings of the whats, whys, and wheres in our universe and to fulfill our part of which the succession of synergetic aggregate systems that our universe, and maybe others, is composed.

Hide and Seek

I started to seek because they have something to hide.
I followed my intuition and it opened my mind.
Ah, its mind they are hiding from others to find.
Their sinister facade is keeping us blind.
Our misused philanthropy we've been living since birth
rewards us with calamity while expanding their worth.
Our non – peripheral awareness has lead us to think
it's not they who're at fault, its nature that stinks.
The synchronized financial enemas that colonic our nests
thirsts parasitic prosperity of those battling for best.
Though their synthetic parallel has made everything so well,
It's non – symbiotic and will be ending in hell.
Right now we're preoccupied with its tastes and its smells,
but it's a cellophane atmosphere, and you can bet they won't tell.
Mother Nature has plans to prosecute our courses
for pillaging her lands that provide our resources.
Because we are nature, they expect to be pardoned
and left to destroy, like gophers in the garden.
Most don't know what's up because power keeps them down.
Do you think I'm crazy, take a look around.
I will continue to seek as long as they hide.
I'm told to ignore it for it will just make you cry.
What will make us all cry is that, when Mother Nature sees fit,
she will turn on all of us with her own game called
                    "Tag you're it".

Harmony

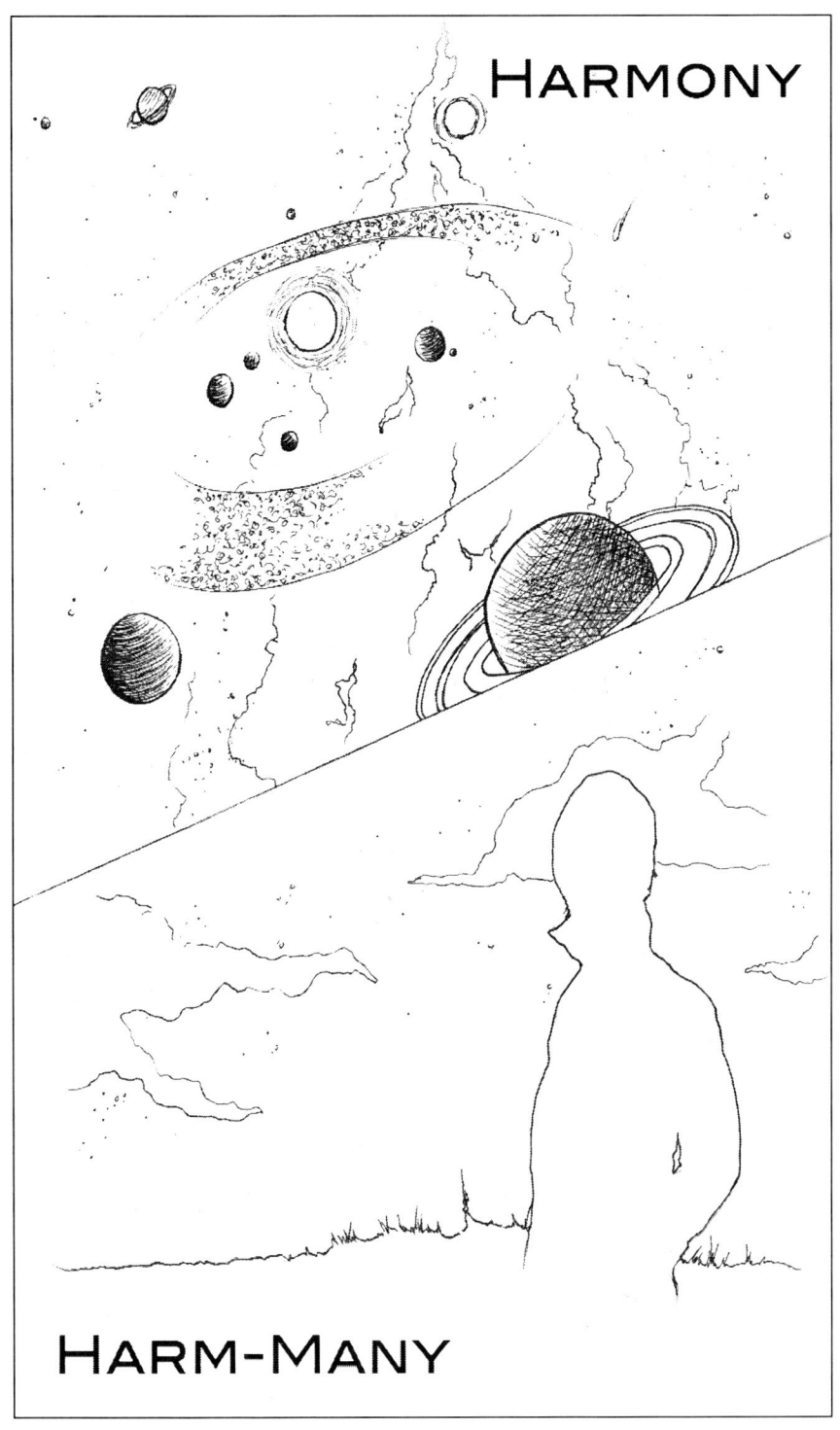

Harm-Many

Re – Cap the Crap

I want to place emphasis on certain things with this chapter. Though I am satisfied with my explanations of what compels me, I could have made this book considerably longer than it is, but I didn't want that to be something to stop someone from reading it. Eventually, I will write books on certain chapters that are in SIGNALS. This book is a positive attempt to get people to realize and address the negative. It describes quite accurately how I feel about these ignored negatives. People say that I'm negative. That's true, but my positive side is seen through this message of peace, which is the overall objective of this book. I mean it to be read as information and not so much as satire.

Even though I am happy with my work, many different conversations must be had in order for me to give this same information in different ways. It would add clarity and depth. Having different conversations can refine my points. It can reduce any ambiguity that may be confusing someone. I don't see how people can explain fully and clearly what they have to say in a few comments or in a short conversation. You would have to talk like Bucky, and few would understand you.

If we're gong to carve what people say in granite like we do, we should know clearly what it is they are trying to say. We have preconditioned expectations of what they're supposed to say.

I think it would be easier if we would realize that we can't explain exactly what we mean. We say we can for the sake of our egos and to try to look confident to others, but we really can't.

We need to stop attacking each other with doubt, ridicule, persecution, and myopic contradiction. We shouldn't judge people the way we do. People's expectations of others are greater than they are able to keep themselves. We judge each other with a set of rules no one can keep. Its conditioned thought that keeps us separated. "We should only judge ourselves on the persons we were yesterday". Henry David Thoreau said in *Walden*.

Personally, I get no psychological stimulation from conquering someone mentally or physically or thinking that I'm better that everyone else. That behavior is insecure. I also want to emphasize that I'm not meaning to belittle anyone. When I talk about the logic and reasoning that society accepts as ok, I am trying to put it with a little bit of humor.

I hope it hasn't been perceived that I am a spiteful person. I am to a point, but it shows my anger. I am disgusted that people are so rigid in their thinking. I think it's easier for people to say it's just me instead of admitting the truth. It hurts people's pride too much to admit they are being taken advantage of by people we are supposed to be able to trust. Everything we are taught has different ways of interpretation and explanation. It is up to us to learn as many of them as we can so we don't become bias to one way of thinking. We have the final say as to what we believe.

Virginia Wolf urged people to move beyond the formal railway line of a sentence. James Joyce said that sentences and paragraphs are like Einstein saying, "Time is relative to the observer". So too are sentences and paragraphs when read by different readers at different times and different places. A lot of explanations are close but differ subtly. This can be a good thing because I have found that different books are good at explaining things differently. Something that I couldn't understand from one person's explanation becomes clear when explained by someone else. Sometimes perspectives and explanations can differ greatly, however, and sometimes it's on pretty big topics. Where you find these discrepancies is a good place to focus your questions. It is where a different perspective can generate conversation and give new ideas.

Also, to repeat again, I am very disappointed in society for ignoring the way things are. I have indescribable disgust for people who have no legitimate excuse for their actions, the people who show just how far capitalism can go. The "that's nature" excuse, not reason, is going to lead to a rude awakening that is not hard to see. It would not please me to see a mutiny occur. It would be terrible if everything fell apart. Life would be miserable for the have – nots only. I really wish that I could go way out into the forest, even if I have to live harshly. That's how unhappy I am in this system, but the men in white coats with their butterfly nets would come get me. They would consider me to be a stray sheep. I feel I am no longer a soldier in the army of social robots and naive public puppets. What's killing me is trying to stop what's killing us. I say again that I need to address what bothers me, but I shouldn't dress in it.

I have been told I should be put on anti – depressants. If I didn't know what was bothering me, I would consider it, but I know what bugs me. Even though it messes with my head, I refuse to get help, for my mind anyway, from a system that I feel is a big contributor to my depression and anger. All they would do is put me in some standardized diagnostic category and run me through a system that I don't agree with in the first place. Asking this system for help would be like asking the bully who would take your milk money for a loan. What I tell people is don't try to change me, you will only make me not like you. Just sit back and watch, that's all I basically do, and I am the one living it!

It is totally unacceptable to accept the way things are as unchangeable. Fair and legitimate existences can happen because I can see them in nature, but we choose a greed and dominant existence. It's nature, isn't it, so we shouldn't feel guilty. No, we should feel guilty. It's nature, but we are supposed to have risen above "instinctive act".

High powers exploit the discoveries or inventions by others of the past and in the present. The people who contributed the life – bettering discoveries are the ones who should get the biggest rewards. Big companies should only get amount x, and that's a lower case x, for their needed but less significant part in developing the products of our advancements. No matter what we do to confront abuse and deception, they give us some B.S.F. excuse. They use mind games and the money tool to keep us in check. They give us the "Oh…well…" introduction to their reasoning and explanations of problems or adversities in something they are trying to initiate, maintain, or cover up in society. The deepest well ever dug by humans is the "Oh…well…" They will say whatever will protect their socially drawn blood money. It's clear unseeable blood when I try to show it to society. They are so programmed, they can't see it, but it is very red when it drips from the subliminal puncture in the jugular vein of social accomplishment and from our later – in – life nest egg building attempts.

Money should not be an issue when it comes to the welfare of humans, especially the children, but right now it is locked up in the capitalistic battles of the so – called "fittest to survive." There's Trillions of undeserved dollars out there due to capitalism or other ways. I think there should not be any Billionaires. All undeserved levels of living should be stopped, and a significant amount of the money should go to children, the elderly, and the handicapped. Higher awareness is making ridiculous amounts of money because there is a feeding frenzy on the weak and unaware. "Ill" – legitimate rewards are proportional to the level of one's abilities in this accepted legal pillage system that is "capitalism". It is definitely a "do as we say not as we do scenario," which makes it skewed toward "those in the know" in society. If we're not careful, they will use the homeless signs that say, "Will work for food" for job openings: HELP wanted – must work for food.

If regulation and restrictions were properly practiced, they wouldn't have to try to regulate societies through structured oppression to the point at which our minds and bodies are adversely affected. If we could have put in place, as technology advanced, objectives and goals of earth protection and human resources respect right from the start, then we wouldn't know any different. Our standard of living would still have gotten much better as time went on. We would be using technology that we are eventually going to have to adopt into our present existence once we realize that a symbiotic relationship with earth and each other is a necessity. Just because we aren't considerate of the earth right now, and we lack human respect, doesn't mean we should continue to behave in this manner.

I hope this book triggers people to search and explore their own minds to whatever level they see fit. I just hope they don't make a "not at all" effort. Let it be your psychological activation energy. I want people to start putting life in front of the world. It is a team effort, but you don't even have to be on the first or second string to play. If you are able to catch an idea and run with it, we need you when you can play.

One of the plays in our playbook is the quarter back sneak. We're going to sneak back all the quarters they snuck out of us in the first place. I know we should dog pile them but that could have adverse consequences. It is time to trim the fat off the cat. Whatever replies I get from the people who read this book, good or bad, I will either file or mount it on the wall with the caption, "I was heard."

To my Lost Love

When you come to me out of the darkness of my lonely but restful nights, in dreams that I fear from knowing you could appear, I forget my conscious inflictions from you when we meet, and I feel only the synchronizing vibrations of our once joining hearts in harmony with our images, lasting only for a dream's moment.

It awakens me, thinking I will find you there, dreaming about me. But in your place that I've saved for another lies a reminding emptiness that sends me back to the final day of our love, the day you journeyed to your "masked love" path of life, fated to you when lying to me.

You tear the slowly closing wound on my forever broken heart, releasing a flood of tears that drowns me back to sleep, only surfacing to wade through an emotional day. Then time forgets me back to another night of dreams we should have shared, tragically ending, again, with my awakening to the waiting sorrow.

The Bridge of Time

We can't feel each other, but I see you. Your in the present day, obeying the demands of nature's dictation. You're unable to receive the signals from my time of wanting to belong to a non – dominated, equaled, and forever lasting togetherness. You say you want to be with me, but still you fulfill nature's needs.

I try to cross the bridge of time that separates us from being one and rescue you from your life of unappreciated contributions, the abuse and denial of you, but I am forced to turn back because you are not there to meet me.

I have met some who have broken free of nature's grasp, but I did not respond because of differences in our lives I could not ignore, so I remain alone with hope that one day we will meet.

But, I'm growing older, and, when you are ready for me, I might not be there for you.

When I think of this as being my fate, it makes me so very sad… I am so sad.

About Buck Minster Fuller

Bucky deserves his own part in this book because he has made the biggest contributions to the courses through which my own mind is taking me, comprehensively explaining why things are the way they are and what we must do to change the way things are so we don't exterminate ourselves completely. I want to bring him out of the depths of complication and credit him with being a pioneer in recognizing the possible reasons why we are here and educating us in how to live symbiotically with the earth. He can see the universe in a way not understood by many. I want to increase the number.

B.F. is my confirmer and my shield, my tutor and my comrade in the pursuit of understanding and the wisdom it produces. I thank my brother, Don, for giving me my first Bucky book: *Intuition*. Before reading B.F., I was, and still am, working on my own intuitive understanding by building an inventory of observations and experiences. Bucky came along and contributed his profoundly, insightfulness, foresighted, omni inclusive, omni considerate, properly sequenced progression of increasingly complex explanations and descriptions of why things are the way they are, how they came about, the inter – connected aspects with us, and what we interpret as reality.

Most of Bucky's work is on what humanity must do in order to be a long – term success on earth. One way he does this is with what he calls the "design science dymaxion world." He says, if humans can't make themselves a long – term success on earth, then we probably won't be able to be a success anywhere else. He has a good point about what is worth doing and what isn't. Once something needs to be built or done, we normally say, "How much will it cost to do it?" What Bucky says is, "How much will it cost if we don't do it?" That is the way we should be addressing our issues.

I don't see why money plays such a large role when it comes to making life better. If people are working, then they get x amount of benefits or credits. There is enough that needs to be done that would keep everyone working either in the maintenance or progress of our existence. The "we don't have the money" "ill" – legitimate excuse, not reason, is a ligature on our ignorance because most of us don't know how to prove them wrong. It's an "ill" – legitimate reason for not taking mandatory steps to increase humanity's well – being. The money that should be going to society is locked up in crap – on – all – ism. Money is a way to keep us struggling and under control. They may be successful for a while longer in controlling us, but they will never ultimately control nature as they are attempting to do. My opinion is that man's progress is at nature's expense, and nature's rehabilitation will be at the expense of man." I can't imagine that humans place on earth is to initiate the next mass extinction.

B.F. has helped me broaden and deepen my own understandings through a more synoptic and synergetic awareness. "Synergy" is also a Bucky word, and here's how he describes it:

Synergy is something about a system that can't be seen by looking at any of its parts, the combination of separate things that create or reveal something else.

You can't see mass attraction with only the body, so the earth moon system reveals the synergy of mass attraction.

There's an alloy called chrome – nickel – steel. The superior strength of that combination produces a **Synergy** that can't be seen by testing the strength of an equal amount of any one of these metals by its self. A basic understanding of synergy is not too difficult to grasp but it's not known by many people. It sounds like the definition of a system. They are interconnected, but synergy does deserve to be a word because it is special and separate. We need to gasp the synergetic benefits of people uniting for change. Unity accomplishes more than individuality. Individualism is most important, but it should be complementary with unity, which is also very important. There is also a synergy when generalization and specialization unite. Generalization is needed whether specialists admit it or not. This synergy will be more utilized when specialists stop being biased to conventional wisdom, and most of them stop letting their egos dominate them.

B.F. is very difficult reading. You have to be able to think of many different things at the same time and try to see the interconnectedness of it all. With practice, you may find his writing to be both enlightening and beautiful. Bucky can interpret profoundly. Here are a couple of experts from his book, *I Seem to Be a Verb*.

"I live on earth at present and I don't know what I am. I know I am not a category, I am not a thing – a noun. I seem to be a verb – an evolutionary process – an integral function of universe."

"The most poetical experiences of my life have been those moments of conceptual comprehension of a few of the extra ordinary generalized principals and their complex interactions that are apparently employed in the governance of universal evolution." Like I said before, a generalized principal is how tension and compression always co occur: convex and concave, mass attraction and precession.

I like a couple of explanations he has for his perspective of the universe; "Islands of compression in a sea of tension," "It's an omni – regenerative scenario universe." Carl Sagan has a different idea for explaining the universe. He suggests that maybe our universe is a tiny closed electron orbiting the nucleus of an atom in another universe.

B.F. uses many complex words. When placed in the proper order, those words make up complex sentences, which, in their proper order, make up even more complex paragraphs. Those paragraphs are only part of a topic, which itself is still only a sub – complex to a subject that is only part of another degree of comprehension. If that isn't enough, what he is ultimately trying to convey can only be seen through thought alone, no words. The intuitive, metaphysically generated, evolution propelled, a priori understanding that is in everyone. It's the exploration of one's brain – mind complementary coexistence.

When I try to reach conclusions in connection with my questions, I not only come up with more questions, I come up with multiple – choice answers. That's because there are multiple – choice scenarios. So, I can see why trying to fully explain my thoughts in one book is not complete enough. As I say more than once in this book, it takes different conversations and writings, and then a synoptic overview to see clearer what it is I'm getting at. Bucky's work, like my own, would be best understood if we, the authors, were to read our work out loud. Bucky thinks out loud. At this time I am limited to writing. I'm working on reading and talking out loud. It's all in the delivery, and that's very hard. If your readers can't read a sentence the way it was written to flow, then it can be misinterpreted or not understood at all. It's frustrating that what we are trying to say can be simply put but gets complicated because mind is being crutched by the inadequate brain – arranged dialogue communication medium. Mind has to cope with the limitations of the brain. Remember, the brain has to run your entire body let alone deal with this new, demanding pest called "mind."

B.F. is also my confirmer. He makes very well known the comprehensive deprivation practices of "those in the know." He doesn't sugar coat it or dilute it in order to make it not look that bad or try to justify it to save face. The truth is that the way things are is "ill" – legitimate, unnecessary, and un – evolved.

Bucky died in 1983 with forty – seven honorary degrees. It feels good to have someone on my side with his level of intelligence, accomplishment, and significant evidence supporting my observations. I feel he would support my fight for justice and fairness. In that sense, he is my comrade and shield. *Critical Path* is the book that gave me some assurance.

I know that what I am trying to accomplish with Signals has a much higher probability for future social system applications than thinking I will see results, significant anyway, in my lifetime. I have already seen positive results in individual cases, and that makes me want to keep going, but to be behind one's time is permanent death. To be ahead of one's time, you're only dead temporarily, but Confucius says, "Dead is dead." Right now, my evidence is a priori. Bucky's has a significant amount of aposteriori to his evidence.

It may look like I'm bias to B.F., but I'm not. There are a lot of statements (Einstein has more than one) from other people that I've found to be helpful. I hooked up, to the best of my ability, with Bucky, but my own stuff takes up most of my time.

I have been watching a program called *The Dog Whisperer*. I don't own a dog at this time, but I still extract a lot of information from that program.

The Dog Whisperer, (Cesar Millan) demonstrates very well the ability to use the right words for people and the right actions for dogs at the right time to get the desired effect. I strive to do that in my conversations with people. The wrong words or actions at the wrong time won't get my message across to people. I think very highly of *The Dog Whisperer,* and I suggest you watch it carefully. You can learn information that can be benefited from even if you don't own an animal.

Thank You, Cesar Millan.

A program that I've been waiting to see again is a program on the science channel.

In a series called *Understanding*. There was a topic called "Memes – The minds big bang." I have learned a little about memes, but that particular program was phenomenal. I only got to watch about half an hour of it, and I've never been able to catch it again. I wonder if they took it off the air because it was information they don't want us to know. I wish I could have watched it before finishing this book. I'm sure I'll include it in one of my next books!

I will briefly mention two other people who have had an encouraging effect on me. They are Michael Faraday and Ben Franklin. On some tapes I have called "The Mechanical Universe," from the Annenberg C. P. B. Project, they mention how Faraday and Franklin shared a perfect innocence of mathematics. I think they may have eventually learned math, but maybe not. They show that you don't have to know math or, for that matter, you don't even have to be a scientist to possess understanding. You can still understand and contribute if you just act like Mike, Ben, and many others, including me. Follow your curiosities and interests, and don't fall into conventional interpretation. And, remember,

"Learning is finding out what you already know.

Doing is showing people that you know.

Teaching is telling people they know just as you do.

We are all Learners, Doer's and Teachers," said Richard Bach in *Illusions*.

Mathematics is a very beautiful and useful tool. It is the mechanical, electrical, and hydraulic complementary, but my approach to understanding and explaining doesn't use much math. I would have to virtually devote the rest of my life to learning the mathematics that are probably necessary to explain how I see things, in a cosmic understanding anyway. My mind won't let me focus on too many single things. I actually should say no single things. I am definitely a generalist; that's what I like to do. What I do is needed but is frequently ignored or discredited as being a valid part of knowledge. I will always follow what compels me. I have found that "it's not how much you know but what you know, and how you know it." I added the last part of that statement to and already existing first part.

If something compels you, then you investigate it as you see fit, no matter what. I'm not saying you shouldn't use a conventional approach as a tool, meaning a "tool," just don't be biased to it. It does play its role, and it is greatly needed, but it's highly probable that individualism is how most new ideas are created. I also mean individuals, but I strongly emphasize individualism. Generalization and unconventional individual intuition are the frequently unacknowledged complements to a specialized, accredited existence. It is the unconditioned initiative by an individual's intuitive metaphysical conceptionings, however, that is exclusively accredited for manifesting the psychological synergy that is "wisdom."

I don't talk down mathematics just because I don't know it. I won't attack it or discredit it, not even the specialists that use it. The world would not be as it is today without it. I just can't, and I guess I'm not suppose to, focus all of my attention on one thing for too long. Specialists can. Specialists make the world accessible and usable, but this accessibility and utilization has gotten way out if hand. One of my biggest disappointments has been in our stewardship of the planet and the treatment of its inhabitants, especially our own kind. Out of all of our resources, the one we abuse the most is a renewable resource, and it is the human resource.

As far as B.F. being my tutor goes, he showed me how to be more inclusive, comparative, observative, and considerate to seemingly unrelated things, and to comprehend to a depth not reached by many. He brought me closer to a deeper wisdom sooner. I credit myself, though, for my direction. I've always been a deep thinker, but Bucky definitely played a part in deepening it even further.

I only say "a part" because his stuff is very complex, and I sometimes have a hard time understanding what he is saying. It is very hard for me to tell others about his way of thinking, and I can't be fluent and properly descriptive. This is partly due to my vocabulary. I only like to use words with which I am, to a degree, familiar. I have a hard time choosing the right words, putting those words into sentences, and then saying those sentences at the right time to most accurately convey what I'm thinking.

I'm not saying that I'm not confident or even inferior. I just know my limitations, and I don't have an ego that needs protecting. I can get closer to breaking free of those limitations if I leave my ego out of it. An ego is an adverse side effect of intelligence.

I've spent years trying to clarify what's in my head. Bucky can think out loud on just about anything you can throw at him. I want to emphasize the rarity and magnitude of intelligence it takes to have that ability to the depth he does. I think that, when you have that kind of ability, it comes easier to you, and you don't have to strain yourself as much as other people do when trying to be fluent and complete without ambiguity. Overall, many people contribute to the information pool that I assimilate when exploring, creating, describing, or explaining my own understanding of what something is, what it does, its purpose, or how to will end up. I like to call it "thought tectonics." It is undeniably an accumulation of teamwork efforts that knowledge progression and evolution require, despite the credential stealing that goes on between egos that are demanding appeasement.

When describing B.F., I conservatively say that he is headed in the right direction. It would be bias and ignorant of me to stay he is exactly right. He has inconsistencies, contradictions, out right mistakes and half – seen truths just like everyone else does. Some statements he makes even get me wondering, but I can neither confirm nor deny what he says because I wouldn't know how to argue the point. I think he is digging into his deepest thought abilities, or maybe he is not meaning to be taken too seriously. There should not be any trashcans in science or philosophy. B.F. has some pretty bold statements that offend a lot of people. Gee, I wonder who else is like that. Once you say something that someone doesn't like or agree with, they will more than likely hastily reject you all together. I extract from Bucky's work what will help me with my work. That is what I do with anybody's work. Understanding a lot doesn't have to be difficult. Everything is connected in one way or another. The ultimate explanation will be a simple one. If I could explain everything in just one word, for the physical universe or the psychologies of people, that word would be "equilibrium." In abstract, the terminology would be "A and B interacting makes C." C, being another A or B, interacts with a different A or B, making another C..... which, eventually, will end up in "equilibrium"

Bucky's work has "simplicity" to his ideas but gets very complicated in his explanations. The fact everything is connected is simple in concept, but just try to explain it. Bucky does a great job, but, as we evolve, so will our understandings and explanations. We only have the "provisional truth" as the Science Channel says, meaning, that we only have the knowledge of what our minds have provided for us so far.

Of course, don't forget about the distortion or misdirection of the truth to what higher awareness wants most of us to know, so protecting their political or religious hidden agendas or the rigors of their "carved – in – granite," biased, conventional wisdom – reasoning.

I wish B.F. were still alive so I could hear his input on some thoughts of mine that ask questions like, since it is widely accepted that we are made from stars, then shouldn't our psychologies and the accompanying physical behaviors mirror or reflect in some way the behaviors or life cycles of stars, either directly or abstractly? Don't stars mirror or reflect the properties and characteristics of the interactions between the atoms and molecules of which stars are composed or of the systems in which those stars are a part of? Don't humans try to reach equilibrium within themselves just like stars do?

If this is true, then maybe, also like stars, atoms and molecules imitate or reveal what is going on at an even deeper level. Maybe, instead of saying at a deeper level, I should say at a more beginning, or elementary level, the unwinding of the synergetic hierarchical complex. I have been going in that direction, anyway.

I can describe myself as being an atom or electron that wants to escape from the environment it's in to an environment better suited for it to reach the equilibrium it needs. If the psychologies and behaviors of people really are related to aspects of other systems, then can't we learn more about atoms, molecules, or other systems just by watching people either as individuals, groups, or society as a whole? Wouldn't this be a way of seeing outside of ourselves?

All systems are trying to reach equilibrium, and are being influenced by the systems that surround them. Don't people show they are trying to reach a psychological equilibrium through their words and actions? Can't great leaders be looked at as the central atom with their subjects and administration being the structure of a molecular complex? I wonder if central atoms treat other atoms like crap just like rulers do to their subjects.

Do atoms, just like rulers, discard an atom or electron (person) when a better atom or electron (person) comes along, or when an atom or electron can't properly fulfill other atom's or molecule's needs? In a non – ruthless sense, I find that I write like that. I try to find the best word for the job, replacing a word when a better word comes along. Maybe words can be compared to oxidation number for atoms, different meanings when used in different circumstances. Grammer isomers or description isotopes.

Here are a couple of other examples of how we mirror or reflect our environment. The early solar system was a very violent place but has quieted down over time. The solar system is still violent, but, compared to yesteryears, it is considerably less violent. It still has its flare – ups, though. Chemical reactions are considerably more active or violent at first; they then become less active as the system gets closer to its new equilibrium, but chemical reactions also have short flare – ups. The history of humans shows a clear sequence of system progression that is very much the same as the previous two descriptions of systems seeking or heading toward a new equilibrium.

Humans show a psychological evolution even though we have repeated the same psychological progression over and over in our past. History repeats its self, but I mean an expanding psychological evolution.

Like the other examples, humans have their behavioral flare – ups, too. Humans' psychology can abstractly be overlain with the physical expansion of our environment and the universe. Human flare – ups are usually caused by an isolated pocket of less equilibrated reactant that's frequently concentrated in a single psychology, commonly called a tyrant, which disrupts the flow toward social equilibrium. The individual psychology could represent an atom or molecule that controls or influences any connected atoms or molecules.

A group's psychology also has its flare ups but could represent a different control or influence on the surrounding and connected atoms and molecules. Humans do demonstrate a psychological imitation of our environment systems. I can see this in our history and in the present day. As systems go from an old equilibrium to a new equilibrium it is not a steady, direct flow. It is like the seasons in which it has a destination but is not direct and smooth. It is fluxually active and never idle. With the seasons, sometimes it seems that Mother Nature shows sympathy by delaying the coming events to give the weak some time to gather their strength. Other times, she arrives unexpectedly to prematurely evict the bounty of weak, or she'll prolong the hardship of those species caught off guard by the premature arrival or late departure of her misdirected punishments.

This is the best explanation I can give at this time of how we mirror or reflect in our psychologies and accompanying actions the physical behaviors of other systems, such as stars or chemical reactions that take place here on earth. I bet B.F. would have something to say about this hypothesis. He would be glad to see that I'm following my own mind and not conventional knowledge or social expectation.

Bucky also profoundly relates the physical to the non – physical but not as I have done here.

Since we have the ability to recognize deep interconnections with other things, as I have attempted to do here, it clearly shows that we can break free of nature's dictation and even the obedience to an even deeper level of cosmic dictation. To me, its pretty compelling evidence that mind is separate from the brain, and that promoting mind development is the path we need to take to holistically understand our previously only pondered questions as to our genesis, purpose, and destination of life's "surreal" role in universal evolution. My utmost deepest thoughts are in trying to find evidence to support my intuition that we also behave in a "dimension fractal inner – patterning, or inter – patterning" or a "dimension transition relative inner – patterning, or inter – patterning" manner. Those are the best words I have at this time to describe my present and future metaphysical conceptionings and explorations. I have a long way to go.

Einstein has his "space – time." When I'm in my deepest thought, I like to say I'm in "spaced – time." I'm so far away in my thought experiments that "spaced – time" is the only way I can describe it. My brain gets left behind but my mind is very active. Albert Einstein also helped me better comprehend when he said three things. He said, "Imagination is more important than knowledge." It's true. Knowledge is built and propelled by the imagination. Knowledge is for now and is feedback for the imagination. The imagination progresses the now. He also said, "If you want to understand something, put it in a form you can understand." The absorption of or exploration through a problem or curiosity becomes easier when you understand. Thirdly he said, "The universe is a non – simultaneous, partially over – lapping, synergetic aggregate of energy – transforming events, ordered by angle and frequency."

I learned this last statement through B.F., but I can't find in which book I read it. It is complete and simple.

To start concluding this chapter, if you like very deep thought, and you aren't biased to conventional wisdom, then I suggest you investigate R. Buck Minister Fuller. I suggest *Critical Path* for more earthly issues, such as his dialogue about power, the "speculative" history of humanity, or evidence of individual or group wrongful manipulation and deceit of societies. It also has his "Self – disciplines of Buck Minister Fuller."

Secondly, try his book *Intuition*. If I tried to describe that book, I couldn't do a proper job, and it would take a few pages. A few words might be deep, inclusive, complete, descriptive, considerate, poetic, difficult to follow but goddamned beautiful when I can. I wrote some excerpts from both of these books. It's the next chapter. If you can hook up with either of these two books, then try *Ideas and Integrities*. There's a chapter in it called "Total Thinking." That's all I can tell you.

B.F. also has books called *Synergetics I,* and *Synergetics II*. The second is the extended issue. It's about explorations in the geometry of thinking. *Ideas and Integrities*, and *Synergetics* are some of the most complicated books on the face of the planet as far as synoptic, all – inclusive reading goes.

Remember, however, if you have a hard time reading Bucky, don't give up. Skim through, and you'll find places to ride the Bucky wagon. Start with that, and you will gradually be able to digest more as you read and learn how he writes. When you think a sentence is supposed to be ending, it's not; it's probably just beginning. Have a dictionary ready because you'll need one. I use Webster's ninth and tenth collegiate dictionaries. A way to further describe how B.F. writes goes as follows, just to let you know what you're in for. Instead of saying, "pass the salt," Bucky would say, "pass the naturally and abundantly occurring, evaporatively – produced, water – soluble, crystalline – structured, ionic – bonded, diatomic, multi – purposed, food – enhancing substance over to me please.

B.F. will be more recognized, which he deserves, as his do and don't behaviors of human activities reach critical importance, like they are right now. We need to realize that we must adapt to the environment, and not the other way around. It must be a symbiotic relationship and non – parasitic. Bucky has been recognized for his influence or indirect contribution to Nano – technology. It is through his geodesic dome, and the C60 molecule. They named them "Bucky balls," " Bucky tubes," or, collectively speaking, "Fullerenes."

The system we use now needs the environment to stay the same in order for us to work most efficiently, and that's impossible. Any fluctuation or permanent change upsets our system.

Why do we have to be at or near full throttle all of the time? Life is meant to be enjoyed, not labored through.

Our providers and leaders, to me, look at fluctuations in our systems as a way to complicate the hell out of things to keep us preoccupied so we don't find our minds and realize that the way things are is unjust, and that mind can take you on the best rides of your life without having to physically go anywhere or spend any money. Let your imagination go by letting your intuition flow through the info from your subconscious know. Inheritively and inherently your wisdom will grow, and, consequently, their cover you'll blow.

We should only use nature as a way of learning how to deal with the environment and such, not how to deal with others. The latter should exist in our memories when we reflect back on the way things used to be. We must psychologically break free of nature's dictation so we can legitimately continue fulfilling our place in the universe.

As you steer a course through your waters of understanding, your course may look like a winding river, but, as you learn, your course will straighten. Then, with time, you will one day find you have broken free from the confines of the river of forced ignorance, or learning beginnings, and you are sailing on the seas of wisdom. Its depth is not yet known. Bucky can lend you his boat of understanding, but he will also tell you that you have your own boat…use it.

Excerpts from Buck Minister Fuller Books

Critical Path:

If any citizens start making their own automobile – powering alcohol, the "revenuers" will have to pounce on them just as they do on those making moonshine "likker."

The world's power structures have always "divided to conquer" and have always "kept divided to keep conquered."

On personal integrity hangs humanity's fate. You can deceive others, you can deceive your brain – self, but you can't deceive your mind – self, for mind deals only in the discovery of truth and the interrelationship of all truths. The cosmic laws with which mind deals are incorruptible.

The ruling society's powers assume human masses to be universally ignorant, and accredit them with having only muscle and dexterity value.

The invisible power structures behind the visible king first patronize and help to develop the artist – scientist advanced environment breakthroughs but always go on ever more selfishly to overexploit the breakthroughs.

It seems clear that between 200 B. – C. and A.D. 200, a deliberately planned policy was adopted by the combined supreme political and religious power structure of that period, which undertook the conditioning of the human reflexes to misconceive and mis – see, or mostly not see at all, the macro – micro cosmic systems in which we live. Their success drew the curtains on science for 1700 years.

Assuming that the people would be benefited by what their representative's government did with the money it borrowed, the people gladly would be taxed in order to pay the money back to the landowners with interest. This is where a century – and – a – half – long game of "wealth poker" began with the cards being dealt only to the great landowners by the world power structure.

To hold their distributors, GM, Ford, and Chrysler deliberately manufactured a few of their mechanically well – designed parts with inferior materials that were guaranteed to deteriorate electrolytically or otherwise.

The "know how" club, monopolized by lawyer capitalism, was a very tight club. Furthermore, the nonmember four billion plus human beings knew nothing about the invisible micro – macro, non – sensorally – tune – in – able reality. Large private enterprise had now hired all the "know how" scientists and engineers. They seemingly could keep the public out of their affairs forever.

We have two fundamental realities in our universe: the physical and the meta – physical.

I am concerned with the unique cerebral faculties, conceptual metaphysical, and physical articulabilities integral to, and operative only within the inventory of, one single individual human's functioning.

Ecology is the world – around complex inter – complementation of all the biological species' regenerative inter – cycling's with nature's geological and meteorological transformation recycling. Society discovered ecology only when its economically sidewise discards of unprofitable substances became so prodigious as to pollutingly frustrate nature's regenerative mainstream inter – support.

Having no academically earned scientific degrees, I could not qualify for membership in any scientific societies and could therefore not publish my discoveries officially in their journals.

The worth of a patent is not established by the merit of the invention but by the expertness with which its claims of invention are written.

All the mystery inherent in all human experience, which, as a lifetime ratioed to eternity, is individually limited to almost negligible twixt seeings, glimpses of only a few local episodes of one of the infinite myriads of concurrently and overlapping operative sum – totally neverending cosmic scenario serials.

One of the most fantastic capabilities of the mind is that of complex inter – patterning recognition.

Pure science means setting in order the facts of experience and, from there, deducting generalized principals if and when they manifest. Applied science means the development of technological procedures for objective employment of a plurality of the generalized principles.

Human continuance depends on the individual's integrity of speaking and acting only on the individual's own within – self – intuited and reasoned initiative.

• • •

> *If all good people were cleaver,*
> *and all cleaver people were good,*
> *the world would be nicer than ever*
> *we thought that it possibly could.*
> *But somehow, 'tis seldom or never*
> *that the two hit it off as they should;*
> *for the good are so harsh to the cleaver,*
> *the cleaver so rude to the good.*
> — Elizabeth Wordsworth

A POET'S ADVICE
A poet is somebody who feels and who expresses their feelings through words.

This may sound easy. It isn't. A lot of people think or believe or know they feel, but that's thinking or believing or knowing; not feeling. And poetry is feeling, not knowing or believing or thinking.

Almost anybody can learn to think or believe or know, but not a single person can be taught to feel. Why? Because whenever you think or you believe or know, you're a lot of other people, but the moment you feel, you're nobody but yourself. To be nobody but yourself in a world which is doing its best, night and day, to make you everybody else means to fight the hardest battle which any human being can fight and never stop fighting.

As for expressing nobody but yourself in words, that means working just a little bit harder than anybody who isn't a poet can possibly imagine. Why, because nothing is quite as easy as using words like somebody else. We all of us do exactly this nearly all of the time, and whenever we do it, we are not poets.

If, at the end of your first ten or fifteen years of fighting and working and feeling, you find you have written one line of a poem, you'll be very lucky indeed. And so, my advice to all young people who wish to be poets is to do something easy, like learning how to blow up the world, unless you're not only willing, but glad, to feel and work and fight till you die.

Does this sound dismal? It isn't. It's the most wonderful life on earth. Or so I feel.

— E.E. Cummings

• • •

Intuition:

Because the physical characteristics of an aggregate's separate components and their respective sub – motions cannot explain the behaviors of their progressively encompassing and progressively complex systems, we learn that there are progressive degrees of synergy, that is to say, synergy – of – synergies, which means complexes of behavior aggregates holistically unpredicted by the separate behaviors of any of their sub – complex – aggregates. Because mass attraction does not predict precession, each sub – complex – aggregate is in itself only a component behavioral aggregation within an even greater behavioral aggregation whose comprehensive behaviors are never directed by the component – aggregates alone. It is, furthermore, in experimentally disclosed evidence that there is a synergetic progression in universe, a hierarchy of total complex behaviors entirely unpredicted by their successive sub – complex's behaviors.

Though popularly unrealized, it is in experimental evidence that the origins of science are inherently immersed in an a priori mystery.

Knowledge is of the brain, wisdom is of the mind.

Again and again, step by step intuition opens the doors that lead to designing more advantageous rearrangements of the physical complex of events we speak of as the environment, whose evolutionary transition ever leads toward the physical and metaphysical successes of all humanity.

If all humanity attains planetary successes, central to that attainment will be the magnificently regenerative power of the Greeks' intuitive synergetic spontaneity of thought.

The non – simultaneity and dissimilarity of the complementary inter – patterning pulsations integrate to produce the complex of events we sensatorially identify as reality.

What we call seeing is the interpretive imagining in the brain, of the significance and meaning, of the nervous system reports of an assumed outsideness of self.

From my viewpoint, by far the greatest challenge facing young people today is that of responding and conforming only to their own most delicately insistent intuitive awareness of what the truth seems to them to be as based on their own experiences and not on what others have interpreted to be the truth. Regarding events in which neither they nor others have experienced based knowledge. This means not yielding unthinkingly to "in" movements or to crowd psychology.

Witnessing the mistakes of others the preconditioned crowd reflexingly says, "Why did that person make such a stupid mistake?" We knew the answer all the time. So effective has been the non – thinking, group deceit of humanity that it now says, "Nobody should make mistakes," and it punishes people for making mistakes. In love – generated fear for their children's future lives in days beyond their own survival, parents teach their children to avoid making mistakes lest they be put at a social disadvantage.

Thus, humanity has developed a comprehensive, mutual self – deception and has made the total mistake of not perceiving that realistic thinking accrues only after mistake making, which is the cosmic wisdom's most cogent way of teaching each of us how to carry on. It is only at that moment of humans' realistic admission to themselves of having made a mistake that they are closest to that mysterious integrity governing the universe.

There are probably myriads of successful human mind counterparts on consciously operating plants, despite greater myriads of failures.

Universe is the aggregate of all of humanity's consciously apprehended and communicated experiences, which aggregate of only partially overlapping events, is sum – totally a lot of yesterdays plus an awareness of now.

Scientists have learned that the human brain is a vast communication system able to record and retrieve information at varying rates of lag. The brain is a special case concept communicating system very much like a television set. It's not just a telegraph wire, not just a telephone, its omni sensorial conceptual as well. It deals with our optic receipts as well as our hearing, our smelling and our touching. In effect, we have a tele – sense station wherein we receive the live news and make it into a video tape documentary.

In our brain studio, we have a myriad of such videoed recordings of the once live news, all of which we hold in swiftly retrievable storage.

You are the T – V studio's production director surrounded by many repeater cathode – ray tube sets. You say, "What is going on here," as you view, hear, smell, feel, the news. Can I recognize this scenario? Have I seen it before, or anything like it?

Your phone – headed assistants search the files and plug in any relevant documentaries.

In any television station studio, the director intuitively sorts and selects source sequences from out of the myriad of relevant sceneries live or replayed, putting the subject at long range, in full environmental perspective, and now at close range scrutinizing some detail. Other cameras have their lenses aimed at static photographs, and others still feed in clip from a host of yesterday's documentary footage.

The director also has available to him imaginarily invented footage as well as yesterday's experience clues, which may be appropriately considered at various stages for mixing in with the news. Out of all this comparative viewing, the director then selects an appropriate action scenario to be taken now in view of both the new challenges and the documentary reminiscences.

I hope these very few excerpts will generate an interest to further explore Bucky and yourself. It will help you to read from the virtual book of forbidden knowledge that is, for now, only communicated between "those in the know" people through what I call "the unspoken word."

Signals from Within

To be able to explain most clearly my thoughts in this section, some years must pass. The reason I'm talking now is because of the intuitive similarities between "Signals Ascend from Within" and this section. My observations and experiences in the first section have been validated by a priori. This told me that my intuition and analytical capabilities were worth employing when trying to figure out something I have a hunch about or something I don't understand.

As stated in the introduction, this section is about my cosmic understandings, and I don't have nearly as much time into it as I do with the previous section, but I'm going to write about what I have so far. Not only to exercise my intuition again but also to spark some interest in others to investigate and explore their own minds in a metaphysically intuitive and mostly unconventional way. I feel I will be in the "mental scaffolding" stage, (as Dr. David L. Goodstein describes it,) for quit awhile longer but, I have enough material to fill a few pages anyway.

Before I start talking about my curiosities and perspective of what's out there, outside our "Spaceship earth," as B.F. calls it, I want to talk in – depth about specialization and generalization. Specialization has generated a bias rigidity when it comes to acceptance or even an acknowledgement of unconventional metaphysical or general exploration or of a new perspective in science. I have no credentials, so I have to carry an extra – resistant, anti – ego, anti – bias, and anti – rigidity shield. This rigidity of specialization has conditioned us to over – look, or discredit, the much needed metaphysical and generalization aspects of knowledge. Metaphysical and generalized thought has a significant role in science. I feel they are as equally important as specialization when looking at the synoptic over view of our accomplishments.

Tony Rothman, who is the author of *Instant Physics,* says, "Scientific thought stems from philosophical ideas." Philosophical ideas have a generalized component with a metaphysical core. Generalization is a good initial viewpoint. It can guide you around until you can find a relevant focus to what your objective is if you have one. It starts to become specialization the more you single out and focus on one "specific" thing only. There is no definite boundary between generalization and specialization. It does have a "gray" area. I'm not saying that all specialists are rigid; I just want them to exercise their more than likely untapped metaphysical abilities. Most don't, and I bet they would be good at it.

Bucky has opinions on specialization, but I think he goes too far. I agree when he says, "The best teacher is experience outside the classroom," but he says, "Classrooms are a concentration of desk prisons." I think the classroom is very important. Bucky has a quotation about specialization that I really like. It is from his book, *I seem to be a verb*. "Extinctions occur when the over specialized species is confronted with a major surprise, an evolutionary event with which it's specialization, (won at the cost of general adaptability), cannot cope." Maybe a reason he attacks specialization is the fact that the ego and pride of specialists have generated a bias favoring specialization, ignoring the inclusive, nonspecific, generalized metaphysical conceptioning that is significant to finding and following the critical path of our fragile existence. I want to unite specialization and generalization because these two things together manifest a synergy important to making sure we're not missing something important, which we still do though because of our "still in infancy" understandings. Specialization and generalization together are the double helix of knowledge, but we don't utilize the two as we should. Rigid specialist conventionalism spills over into unconventional conceptualism and attempts to direct thought so to not upset the conventional inventory of data they have mistakenly carved in granite. Generalization generates knowledge spores through an intuitively sparked metaphysical awareness, exploration, and reasoning. It remains metaphysical until you can tune in and isolate something that relates to what you're trying to understand to a point at which you have a pencil in your hand trying to find the mathematics to explain it or a specific experiment to back up your hypothesis, but don't forget there is a gray area, however.

I am disappointed we don't recognize the importance of the metaphysical and general aspects of understanding. Metaphysical conceptioning generates wisdom, which is a product of mind.

Knowledge is of the brain and wisdom is of the mind, the weightless metaphysical mind," says B.F.

Specialization is an in – depth look of a specific thing, or system, where generalization is focused on relationships between many things or systems. Generalization is more synoptic than specific. Specialists, I think, are more likely to have an ego that dominates them, and it makes them biased to a specialist's point of view. An ego is an adverse side effect of intelligence. An ego is also anti team effort and credit. An ego is an insecurity in people, but it doesn't necessarily mean that person is insecure in other ways.

Unfortunately, generalists can get to a point at which they lose the interest of those listening. The listener's belief also deteriorates. This is because generalization involves looking at the difficult to see interconnected relationships of a lot of different things at one time, and that is very hard to do. People will put down what they don't understand or can't do. Specialization is more observable. For instance, we really wouldn't have anything if there weren't those men and women who devote virtually all of their time to one "specific" thing. The world would not be as it is now without specialization. Technology is a fantastic thing, isn't it? Too bad we abuse it, take it for granted, and use it to control others.

Since specialists spend little to no time in the much – needed realm of generalization and metaphysical thought, they dismiss it as being a valid part of scientific thought. Not really knowing that the essence of what they're working on was more than likely metaphysically conceptualized earlier in scientific history, but keep in mind that a lot of scientific discoveries are made by accident.

"Name the greatest of all inventors: accident," said Mark Twain.

It is easier for a specialist to prove his or her point than it is for a generalist. So, the crowd tends to lean toward believing the specialist's explanation or interpretation of a given phenomena.

Metaphysical and generalized thought will be more widely accepted and utilized as mind evolves, and the unnecessary ego goes away, and power structures stop diverting smart people from exercising their generalization abilities by channeling most of their brilliance into one "specific" thing. I've noticed that the really great people are masters at both metaphysical and general conceptioning, and they also have very good specialization abilities. They recognize the importance of metaphysical intuition and general "synoptic" exploration. They can also make those a priori understandings aposteriori by support of an experiment or by mathematics, which take more specialization qualities. You know who some these people are: Newton, Galileo, Einstein, and the lesser known or recognized Buck Minister Fuller. B.F. is very diverse in figuring out and understanding problems. He is very insightive, foresighted, inclusive, and complete. He is, by far, my favorite. He is accurately described as the Leonardo da Vinci of our time.

Even with these brilliant minds, I still quote a statement of mine that says, "Skepticism increases when describing yesterdays, tomorrows, the untouchable, and the unseen." It can keep some of our egos in check by letting us know that there is a lot more to it than of what we are aware. I know there is a lot more to what I try to explain. I am mostly a generalist. I am not able to focus my attention too long on one thing only, but I can "sieve" out and arrange into a detailed explanation what my thoughts are. That, in a sense, has a specialized component. A way I use my generalization technique to make things more observable, understandable, absorbable, or explorable is that I consider every entity to be a system. This takes some of the overwhelming complication out of trying to integrate everything together as they appear in reality. So, calling things "systems" instead of what they are helps me to be less confused. Also, learning becomes easier when you know how to "take notice," seeing subtle things that can't be noticed when trying to understand too much at one time. Taking notice can break down walls.

Utilizing the capabilities of your minds' learning abilities flows by itself when you let it. If you have trouble learning, don't try to learn, just watch it, or read it, and wait to see what it is you absorbed, maybe it will be nothing at first. You may only remember the effect it had on you. Watching programs that are geared for kids is a good way to learn the essence of things. Generalization is a good postulate for learning. If you get confused, just remember that confusion is a non – synchronicity between brain and mind. Confusion will reduce as you learn but may never completely go away. It hasn't in me yet, but I have found that metaphysical conceptioning and generalized observing have reduced my confusion considerably.

I like my metaphysical and generalization abilities, but at this time they are only personally rewarding. At least I have recognized this so I can more efficiently do what I am good at, which is trying to contribute a food source, give support, evolve, or draw question to an existing accepted understanding or hypothesis. I have no credentials. I'm my own best audience, and what I say is a priori. I'm not saying I'm inferior or unconfident. Recognizing my limitations can help me break free of those limitations. One limitation everyone has is that, the more you know about one thing, the less you can know about another. Not many can be good at everything. I have confidence with what I say, and I believe that true confidence does not include an ego or ignorance. An ego sours teamwork efforts. People who have an ego brag about themselves. If what you say or do is worth bragging about, people will brag for you.

The best results come from an aggregate of different perspectives. A unity, or polymer of individualism, but not to the point of biased conventionalism. This can create a synergetic perspective that can't be achieved by one person interpreting each factor involved in understanding a given problem. Using conventional analysis keeps us from fully understanding a problem. Bucky describes this very profoundly with a statement I read in *"Critical Path"*, from his book, Synergetics, Explorations in the Geometry of Thinking:

Conventional critical path conceptioning is linear and self under informative. Only spherically expanding and contracting, spinning, polarly involuting and evoluting orbital system feedbacks are both comprehensive and incisively informative. Spherical – orbital critical feedback circuits are pulsative, tidal, importing and exporting. Critical path elements are not overlapping linear modules in a plane, they are systematically inter – spiraling complexes of omni inter – relevant regenerative feedback circuits."

In this statement he is describing a comprehensive progressive or evolutionary analysis, observing something from all angles, comparing and interconnecting it with relevant or irrelevant internal or external systems. He is not being biased to a strict order of analysis. Individual intuitive and metaphysical analysis joined with others of the same approach, creating, discovering, evolving, and unbiasedly interacting. Basically, it flows when you let it. I noticed that explanations of the physical environment, such as a complex of inter – related, cooperating, sub – complex, aggregate systems can also be used as an explanation of the realm of thought.

The main reason I continue on my path of universal understanding is because even people who have credentials, documented, demonstrated, or both, argue about what's right or wrong on some pretty important topics. If they are so certain about our understanding of something, and they talk like they are, then shouldn't bright people, especially the specialists, agree on topics that could have a significant importance to the accuracy of something else?

Another reason I feel confident about what I say is that, throughout the history of knowledge, it has frequently been said, "It's not what we previously thought." Then, they say, "But now that we have this new information, we are certain we are correct." Then, x amount of time goes by, and we say again, "It's not what we previously thought." I think they do that because of blind confidence or an ego that dominates them. Whatever they can't fill in with direct or indirect evidence, they fill it in with what Dr. David L. Goodstein calls "The scholarly imagination." That's not a bad thing just so long that the reason they do it is to fill in the gaps to complete the story and not to stroke their egos or to make them look smarter than they really are. They should frequently remind us of their possible inaccuracies so we don't carve what they say in granite.

I only want to criticize scientists for saying, "It's not what we previously thought," when they're deterministic and conclusive about what they're talking about. I don't mean to criticize them when they say, "It's not what we anticipated."

From this viewpoint, I feel that there is plenty of room for amateur interpretation and explanation. Whatever I come up with as an explanation for something, I know it's only part of a bigger something else that has its own explanation, and so on.

Yogi Berra made a comment that describes our over confidence with understanding. He said, "What gets us into trouble is not what we don't know but what we know for sure that just ain't so." B.F. says in *I Seem to Be a Verb*, "Science isn't very receptive of new perspectives because it is detrimental to their backlog of information." Amateur perspective is from unconditioned learning. Even though we have progressively gotten smarter, we are still traveling through knowledge with one foot on the path and one in the mud.

What generates my understandings is nature. I use nature, as do others, as my envelope or as boundaries for what I will accept as an explanation of the universe as a whole or any of its sub – aggregate, aggregate systems. I even use nature to observe the possibility of a multi – universe scenario.

I speak either directly, abstractly, metaphorically, or implicitly. Open your mind to perspective and intuition, and place less importance on conventional wisdom. Here are some examples of my analysis and reasoning using nature as my example.

Life started out as a single celled organism. Sounds plausible, a man's sperm or a woman's egg can abstractly represent a single cell that evolves into something completely different in appearance and function. Science has a chronology for the development of life from a single celled organism to present day humans, but, in relation to that, I wonder what a sequence would like if they used only visual clues to create a chronology of a "single species" evolution.

Life started out in water. Again, this sounds plausible. We develop in a womb of water and then we emerge from that watery genesis. It is also seen in amphibians. They support the watery genesis theory by going from breathing water to breathing air.

The big bang theory. Briefly, it states that the universe started out as a point of infinitely small size with infinite density. It exploded, and now it's expanding. I look for evidence in nature to support this. I notice that everything starts small and then gets bigger in a physical sense just as the universe is said to be doing.

That's as far as I take it. Something started out small, or smaller, and is getting bigger. To take the big bang all the way back to a singularity seems mathematically directed. There are other phenomena in nature that expand for different reasons. They still start out small but not under the same parameters as the big bang. For example, clouds, river deltas, certain substances reacting, all have different reasons for going from smaller to bigger.

Mathematics is beautiful and phenomenally useful, but I feel that the answer to everything will be made through observations of our environment and not equations. If we were exactly right with our computations, the factors in those computations were correct, and we included all the variables that occur at different times in the life cycle of our universe, then a mathematical explanation would apply. Since we frequently say, "It's not what we previously thought," and this includes people who emphasize that the ultimate explanation will be through mathematics, I believe there are inaccuracies or unknowns that would throw of any mathematical explanation that far in the past or the future. Mathematics works very well for the time frame in which we are, but even in there is error. That is why I believe that the past, present, and future of our universe can be seen by taking a stroll in nature, just so long as our universe system isn't, at a later time, disturbed by an outside universe system. Any outside systems that are playing a part in the course of our universe system at present aren't considered to be "new" inclusions that may make our universe take a "different" path toward a "different" final equilibrium.

I use a biological / universal comparative explanation for my analysis because it is easier to observe. Non – biological concepts can be incorporated into my explanations. I don't want to sound biased to life – oriented explanations. Since we are made to understand our existence, it seems a life – oriented explanation would be what is appropriate, but I won't carve it in granite, or be biased to it. Whatever mathematical explanation they come up with, if correct, should have a way to observe it in nature from a non – mathematical stand point. The Phebonachi sequence, fractal geometry, and the golden section are mathematically explained, yet they can still be observed without knowing math. So, I consider that to be a plus for a physicist's point of view. Also, any universe explanation should be understandable by someone with an average intelligence and on an observable scale and time frame. The catch is that an awareness of synergy is needed in that average intelligence. Synergy is not commonly understood in an average intelligence, but I say "an awareness of synergy," not a full understanding if it, and that does fall into the average intelligence ability. I can't completely comprehend synergy and I've read a lot about it.

There are a few more observations I have about the big bang theory "concept." First, I noticed something that starts out big and then gets smaller, opposite that of a smaller to bigger explanation. It's computers. The first digital computer was huge, but look at it now.

I realized, though, that knowledge of computers started out small and is getting bigger. Another bigger to smaller is generalization to specialization, synoptic to specific, entropy to syntropy. In the last example, entropy is the large and Syntropy is the small. Syntropy starts out small, so maybe these two are interchangeable. To briefly describe entropy and syntropy, entropy is the increasing disorder of a system, and it is what they say the universe is doing. Syntropy is the increasing order of a system. The decay of life after death is entropy, so, quoting Bucky, "where syntropy reigns, life prevails; where entropy reigns, death prevails." Just because there are bigger to smaller observations, it doesn't disprove the predominantly smaller to bigger observations: they coexist. The universe goes out, but gravity goes in. See? Bucky says, "Gravity is compression and the universe expanding is tension."

My second observation about smaller to bigger is that things even get bigger in an evolutionary sense. Over geologic time, the organisms get bigger and bigger, not just in the time they were alive. Look how big the dinosaurs got. Humans have done the same thing. If the environment or the cosmos doesn't knock us down again, life will eventually directly or indirectly meet and maybe exceed those proportions. Maybe the big bang is part of a fractal sequence. This can be an example of my trans – dimensional fractal inter – patterning that I talked about in the chapter, "About

Buckminster Fuller."

The last thing is that I'm wondering if, in humans, since our brain took a different course than that of other animals, humans will stay the same size we are now because the energy that would have went into making us larger got channeled into a brain – mind expansive complementary system unique to all other systems. That statement is a psychological universal comparative observation. I can also see a psychological universal comparison in the way I write. My ideas and explanations proceed from smaller to bigger just like most everything else I see in nature, and in the universe!

Ok, I think I'm done with the big bang. How about a multi – universe scenario possibility? A pine tree produces many pinecones, and those pinecones each have many seeds. Why so many? It's to insure that some of those seeds do what they were designed to do. The chance of a seed falling into the right conditions is slim. Even then, some seeds still don't properly do what the seed was designed to do all the way through adulthood. When it does fall into the right conditions, it tries to propagate through that environment by repeating the same process from which it came. A man's sperm, the eggs a woman produces throughout her life time, pollen, flowers: there are massive excesses of what's needed in all of these. It is to insure that some will do what they were designed to do. You get what I'm saying? How about the universe?

Another observation that suggests a multi – universe is that every system is a system within a system, within a system, within a system…. Anytime you are going out of a system, you're going into another. "You can go in, out, or around a system" says BF. Just because I can't see outside our universe system doesn't mean it stops there and there are no more systems. If you tossed a coin one hundred times and got heads every time, wouldn't you bet the next toss would have a very high probability of being heads even though you haven't seen the toss yet? I'm showing here how I analyze, and I'm not saying any of this is true, but I'm also not saying it isn't, or I wouldn't have written it.

What defines a universe? If there is a definite boundary between universes, then it would be easy to separate different universes, but if there is no definite boundary, how would we tell when we are in another universe? Maybe we could separate them into universal gravity domains like you would identify separate thunderstorms as being different domains of updrafts. With a definite boundary or not, any or all universes are probably just a part of another greater system aggregate complex just as thunderstorms are a part of a greater system. If we were to say that each thunderstorm is a separate universe, it is still only part of the weather phenomena in that region on earth, which is only part of the whole earth weather system. There's that system within a system analogy again. Systems interact and create cycles, so if you say systems within systems, you can also say cycles within cycles, and it's as neverending as systems are unless the universe dimensionally involutes. Then, it will start back at the first system. The adverse synchronizations of system cycles are the cause of earthly disasters.

B.F. says it is an omni – regenerative universe scenario. That's ok for the universe's present state, but what about a beginning or an end? It's out there to be found in nature. One thing about the universe as a whole is that we don't have another universe to which to compare our universe, so that makes our universe more difficult to understand.

The next analysis is on gravity and black holes. When I watch whirlpools and waterfalls, they reveal evidence that I can use in my thought experiments. I throw rocks into lakes, rivers, and whirlpools and watch the ripples that propagate outward. When the flow of the river is strong enough, the propagating waves don't propagate up stream from a fixed reference on the riverbank. They do, however, propagate outward from where the stone hit, but the whole propagating system moves down stream. In a whirlpool that's strong enough, the ripples don't go outside the whirlpool system. They get sucked into the whirlpool and disappear. Both these observations show that black holes can exist. The whirlpool edge reveals the event horizon. The river itself can, too, but you have to imagine it flowing toward the center of a vortex. Also, when imagining the ripples as light waves, a three – dimensional conception model is needed in the observation. The ripples, in abstract, represent light waves slowed down.

All of this abstract, three dimensions out of two dimensions reasoning, yields information not only on black holes, but on gravity in general. The water represents the interstellar medium, or "dark matter." Don't worry, I won't say the "Ilumeniferous ether." The water (interstellar medium) manifests gravity, but it may not have gravity. It moves because of some other reason. It carries matter along like the wind. Any atom in the interstellar medium has gravity, though.

In contradiction, I think it is said that atoms are made up of dark matter, and that dark matter has gravity. We just don't notice it until it's in an observable matter form. I wonder if there are places in the universe where there is a balanced gravity, meaning you're not orbiting around any center of mass. Two different mass centers are playing tug of war with you, a "balanced" gravity state. Would this imply that the "empty space" universe, in abstract, is a liquid, or a solid, and that Bell's Theorem of the universe being a "seamless whole" is correct? To support Bell's Theorem, I think any terminology used to describe any system can be abstractly used to describe another system. I believe everything is connected, especially the physical and the non – physical. For example, the physical stiffness of the interstellar medium can be seen in the psychological rigidity of one person's acceptance, interpretation, or expectations of another person's thoughts or actions.

Gravity is measured by mass, but I'm wondering how a frequency/volume measurement would fit as a gravity measurement. Remember, this is only a thought. I vision the whirlpool as a vibrating rotating volume. A three – dimensional "spherical" volume with its gravity proportional to its volume and its frequency, or something like that. Volume and frequency are the inclusions in the measurement. The frequency would be the average of all the frequencies of the volume, and the volume is just the volume. Higher frequency and the same volume have larger gravity. Lower frequency has smaller gravity. The same thing is true with volume. You can have the same gravity with different volume/frequency ratios.

This popped into my head when I was trying to find a different reason for someone weighing more at the poles than at the equator other than being closer to the center of mass.

What I came up with is that the flow of dark matter at the poles has more of an unaltered course than the dark matter being dragged around at the equator by a spinning earth. If the dark matter is like the wind, then it would be blowing straight down on the top of your head at the poles and more sideways at the equator.

I have some possible contradictions to this that I thought up while scrutinizing my thoughts. The moon doesn't rotate on its own axis, so how does that affect my gravity explanation? How does a frequency to volume analogy fit with a neutron star? I consider these contradictions to be only obstacles in my path of figuring it out. I know I'm in the mental scaffolding stage with it and will be for a long time. It may turn out that this won't be finished by me but will be picked up by someone else down the road.

Dark matter flows because there is frequency. If there was no frequency, there would be no gravity, but I don't think volumes can exist without frequency. I think all frequencies are headed toward "zero frequency equilibrium" for the final state of the universe. A part of me asks the question, is dark matter limiting frequencies to travel at the speed at which they're capable? This means x – rays would be "faster" than radio waves, but dark matter is like a school zone that makes energy waves pile up at the mass/empty space interface.

I also have a common observation that suggests frequency is like a ball in a can. The more times the ball hits the side of the can in a given time, the higher the frequency. Progressively reducing the volume of the can increases the frequency, like a ping – pong ball bouncing between the convergences of a paddle with the table. I think, in physics, they say frequencies are the manifestations of electron energy states. I like my analogies. So, kiddingly, if what I say turns out to have some truth to it, I think dark matter should be renamed "Duaneium." It could box in the periodic table.

If dark matter flows because of frequency, why is there frequency? Maybe it is from dark matter being made into mass, or disassociating mass back into dark matter. It sounds pretty reasonable that matter is made from dark matter because I can see it in nature, plus it is a widely accepted hypothesis in science. It also seems possible that dark matter is just a medium, product, reactant, or catalyst, like in chemistry. Something had to upset the equilibrium of our universe system to get it going.

In chemistry, the direction of a reaction, overall, is from reactant to product. As this is happening, however, some of the product is going back into reactant as the system is equilibrating. Maybe either matter or dark matter is the reversible reaction in a disturbed system coursing toward a new equilibrium. I see that things take the path of least resistance. I bet that applies to things we don't yet understand.

You can see how I use things in the environment that I can see to observe and try to explain things I can't see, either because they are too big, too small, or not observable in a human existence time frame or scale. I've heard a lot of scientists and others say, "The ultimate answer will be a simple one."

So, I say, why not approach it simply? Could it be that all of our scientific reasoning and venturing will wind up being only a lengthy verification of our intuitive conceptioning at the beginning of the manifestation of our wanting to understand our environment, and our place in it? Remember, you don't have to know science to have understanding or to give input on something. There shouldn't be any trashcans in science or philosophy. I think the only requirement should be an average intelligence with an average reasonability. The past, present, and future of our universe can be seen while taking a walk in nature, either abstractly or directly. This means no microscopes or telescopes. The trick is to put your observations in the proper sequence to represent the different stages. This is done in a way that represents how you see things in your own way.

It is a shame that science is so rigid that, even if a hypothesis sounds plausible, there is a high probability it will be discarded if you get the mechanism wrong. One incident describing this involved a man named Alfred Vagner in geology. He had it right that the continents do indeed drift, but he had the mechanism wrong. Continental drift would, years later, lead to the theory of plate tectonics. Sadi Carnot, who lived in the eighteen hundreds, was interested in steam engines. His ideas were ignored from the beginning, but his ideas brought forth the science of thermodynamics. Time was lost mostly because of the rigidities of science or the jealousy of an ego. I say again, there shouldn't be any trash cans in science and philosophy.

Don't be afraid to ask questions that may help you describe you viewpoint. Remember, even if you are exactly right, a lot of people will myopically respond with doubt, ridicule, persecution, or contradiction. It's a conditioned response that keeps us psychologically separated. It is a subconsciously generated control security measure of the psychologically un – evolved, parasitic, so called "fittest to survive." Will these so called "fittest to survive" people still be the "fittest to survive" when there's no one else to be the "fitter to survive" than?

It's funny that, on our coins, it says, "E Pluribus Unum," out of many, one. They're making us a mindless "one," a non – thinking "one," I will never accept what people accept as just the way it is, and that it can't be changed. James Lowen said, "Those who don't remember the past are condemned to repeat it." Let's start remembering our past so we can be united without a political agenda, a unity with synergetic benefits for all. We will ultimately understand why we are here, and, hopefully, we will fulfill our place in the universe.

Thoughts on Time Travel and our objectives toward space

Time travel has been a good topic for me to see how thought experiments can be a good tool for exploring something I'm trying to understand. I have some questions about time travel, and the grandfather paradox starts it off. I know it's widely agreed that this can't happen. I'll assume you know a little about it, but I've never heard one say what is obvious, that the physical requirement needed to create the grandfather paradox image is long gone. Assuming we could place ourselves at an event of the past in question, we would only be able to observe the event, but in no way could we interact with it.

    I wonder what the scene would look like. I don't think we would see things as you would if you were involved in the event. Those light waves travel parallel to the earth, hit other objects, and now carry those images off of which they reflected. This explanation is with visible light. I guess other ranges of light would also change their images if they can be reflected. I think some may only be emission manifest, but I'm not too familiar with that. A top view is what we would see because we are out in space observing the event. Only light waves that travel outward from the earth is what we would see, light waves that didn't run into any stars or planets. Cloudy days, nighttime events, or indoor events are unobservable in a visible light consideration. Get it? This is only a part of it. We would also necessarily have to keep up with the rotation of the earth in order to observe the event.

    Using the speed of light as our speed limit, (I don't want to rattle that cage), for a math problem in time travel, I have found that we would have to travel many times the speed of light in order to observe any event as far in the past as the grandfather paradox. In fact, we would only be able to travel approximately four hours back in time before our speed would have to be faster than the speed of light to maintain a geosynchronous orbit with earth. The way I figured this out is I found how far light travels in twenty four hours. I bent that into a circumference, and then I divided that by 3.14, or pi. That gave me a diameter. I then divided that by two and got a radius.

    Next, I found how log it takes light to travel that radius distance and that told me how far we could travel back in time using the speed of light as our speed limit. One thing I didn't do was subtract the amount of time it takes light to travel the distance of the radius of the earth because the light wave originated at the surface of the earth, not at the center of the earth. I know we would have to travel faster than the speed of light to catch up to an image that is already traveling at the speed of light, so we'll assume that the thought experiment starts out at an event in question. Disclaimer: I'm not a mathematician, but I know that what I came up with is close. Do you understand the concept of what I'm saying?

One more statement is that we would have to travel great distances in order to move around in an event. For example, if you wanted to look at the different faces of a pyramid at a right angle to each face, it would be short a distance to travel if you were close, let's say 1 mile away, to the pyramid. Great distances, however, would separate those right angle views of each face if you were to try to view them from a distance of one thousand miles out from the earth, and, of course, you would need a telescope.

In one thought observation, I imagine the light wave image being spread out because of the larger surface area of a sphere at a distance, but that is when I use a single light wave in the analysis. In reality, though, there are many different light waves being reflected off an object at many different angles, so the image would stay in proportion but would get smaller and smaller the farther you got away from it. Also, there is a part of me that asks the question, can an event be observed in full scale out in space? If we were to travel with the light waves of an event we just witnessed, wouldn't those images stay the same size? Isn't it a matter of your position relative to the event, meaning part of or not a part of it?

I say again, this topic is Time Travel. I don't have nearly the time into my cosmic understandings as I do with my social understandings. I am constantly exposed to what I wrote about in "Signals Ascend from Within," but I only have books, videos, television, and my metaphysical intuition reasoning for my cosmic understandings. I'm not involved in science. I do my best with the vocabulary I have to work with to convey to others my thoughts on a given subject. My exploration of the universe is still in its infancy. I'm going to predominantly follow my mind, but of course, I will include conventional analysis and wisdom.

I think these are legitimate questions and statements. I can go a lot deeper when I use only thought, but then I can't tell anyone. If you ask me about my deepest thoughts I will respond with a statement that St. Augustine once said, "If you ask me I don't know. If you don't ask me, I know." Just a quick thought before continuing: light as a particle, light as a wave? How about waves acting on particles?

Here's something else on time travel in regards to the Big Bang theory. In order to see the big bang event, wouldn't we have to necessarily be outside this universe system to intercept the light waves, if they exist, that make up the Big Bang event? We only see events that are occurring within the volume the universe has expanded to so far, right? Could this mean that we are misinterpreting the distance across the universe in light years to be the age of the universe? The speed of light may be the limit only inside this universe volume. How do we know the universe didn't expand faster initially? We, at least, need to add the time it took the universe to expend to a given volume on to the time it takes light to travel from a source to our receivers. We base a lot of fact on debatable issues, but I am here to question science, not doubt it. I wouldn't know how to doubt it.

Lastly, I would like to say that my time travel analogies are in a literal sense. There is no leaving common sense behind when I analyze. The fact that we interpret what's happening in stars by analyzing its light means that other events, like human activities on earth, are also observable at great distances long after the actual event took place.

Moving on, as tremendously vast as the universe is, I feel x amount of the space budget is being wasted on needless or not so important issues. To me, once the Hubble deep field photographs were seen, an epiphany should have occurred. We should rethink our approach toward exploring the universe. Isn't it one of our main goals to find out if there's life in the universe besides us? The huge number galaxies and the billions of stars in each overwhelmingly suggest that there is. So, looking for planets around other stars, and S.E.T.I. is a waste of money. Even if we do receive a signal, or find other earth like planets, it wouldn't fulfill the "Extraordinary claims require extraordinary evidence" as Carl Sagan says. I support space exploration very much, but we should spend a lot more time on near earth asteroid identification and litigation and on more local environmental issues. I do, however, support colonizing the moon. We need to have a second location for humanity to continue in case of a global disaster occurring here on earth. I have no doubt they will accomplish this goal. These statements are not intended to offend or discredit anyone. Nor, do I want it to look like I know a lot, but I need to say these things.

Another waste of time and money, at least right now, is a manned mission to Mars. We should at least be able to travel ten times the speed achievable now before attempting something like that. Even then, I see no reason to walk on Mars until we can better combat the effects of space and until many earthly issues have been addressed. Our people are starving, and our children are uneducated, but we're going to Mars! Since we insist on going to Mars soon, I have something more to say about it. When we do land on Mars, and there's no doubt in my mind we can do it, what will be our first words? When we landed on the moon, we said, "The Eagle has landed." When we land on Mars, we should say, "The Ego has landed," because it is our ego that is going. Probes and Landers are fine for now. We can do many unmanned missions at the cost of one manned mission. Venus is Earth's past and Mars is Earth's future.

I repeat, I largely support knowledge gained through space – venturing, but, with some things, I feel we are paying for NASA's play time, and we are catering its egos. I'm being facetious but not sarcastic. At times, I think we shouldn't be able to explore space at all when our current situations here on earth are of critical importance to the continuance of space programs, and, more significantly to our existence period.

A final statement about our objectives toward space is that to think that we can send humans into space any farther than our own solar system is ridiculous. We would have to be more physically and mentally evolved before we could even consider that. You don't try to run a marathon when you can't even crawl. We shouldn't even think about running a marathon until we can at least run a short distance. I don't even think we're crawling in space yet. We're just sitting there looking around like a baby who can't walk yet. We need to do a lot more sitting and looking.

Come on, has our ego distorted what's realistic? Why do we need to go to Mars or into the universe in the first place? How would we know that the new place to which we're going isn't worse off than we are here? I see us having x amount of major situations here on earth that are going to test our ability to adapt to a new environment, and we should be focusing more of our efforts in that area. It will be great if someday we can leave earth for an extended period of time, but we have to be here in order to leave! We should dig ourselves out of this black hole on earth before we go digging into black holes in space.

If there really are Aliens, I wish they would give us a humbling awakening and a moral overhaul to exonerate the oppressed. If they need directions, we live on planet pillage, in the milk – me – way galaxy. If aliens do exist, I bet they are from our solar system. Otherwise, they wouldn't need any type of material vessel to move them around.

Why is it we think that we have to take our physical bodies with us when we do leave earth? I feel that, once the powers of mind are more recognized, and utilized, we won't have to physically go here or there. Mind is still in its infancy. Mind has had a very long incubation period. It has taken many baby steps and has just recently, in the past few hundred years, demonstrated it's potential. Through our mind is how we will be traveling deep into the universe or into other universes. So, it doesn't really matter if everything collapses in the modern world. Just so long as we don't wipe out people all together, the mind will continue, though maybe more slowly, on its own evolutionary course toward a much greater universal function. Right now, mind is learning, developing, and practicing for its up – coming cosmic expansion debut.

Up till now, mind has only been able to perform outside the body, to a skeptical live audience, via the metaphysical or through the death of one or more of its mortal anthropomorphic vessels. Minds' true potential and level of existence is hidden in the social and scientific doubt of philosophy, which, to me, is the shock wave that penetrates the periphery to ultimate understanding and wisdom. It cannot puncture the membrane separating the physical and the non – physical, however, because the philosopher must also change dimensions. Science can only poke at the periphery with its provisional truth. Science swings a big sword of doubt, ridicule, and persecution at philosophers that it forged with the time it should have been devoting to inserting the key into the door that is philosophy.

Science looks where the light is, philosophers dive into the darkness of the metaphysical knowing that, if they let their minds unconventionally adjust to the darkness, they will begin to see that there is no such thing as the darkness of the unknown or unknowable. We all maybe separate universes ourselves, existing in another universe that is a synergetic collective of ourselves, which is the physical universe we call "reality."

The next page is of a graphic that needs some explaining. The very big and the very small are related "through abstract." The very big is the very small. The very hot is the very cold. The very fast is the very slow. The very hard is the very soft. This graphic is an example of dimensional – involution, fractal inner – patterning, or fractal inter – patterning.

Perspective

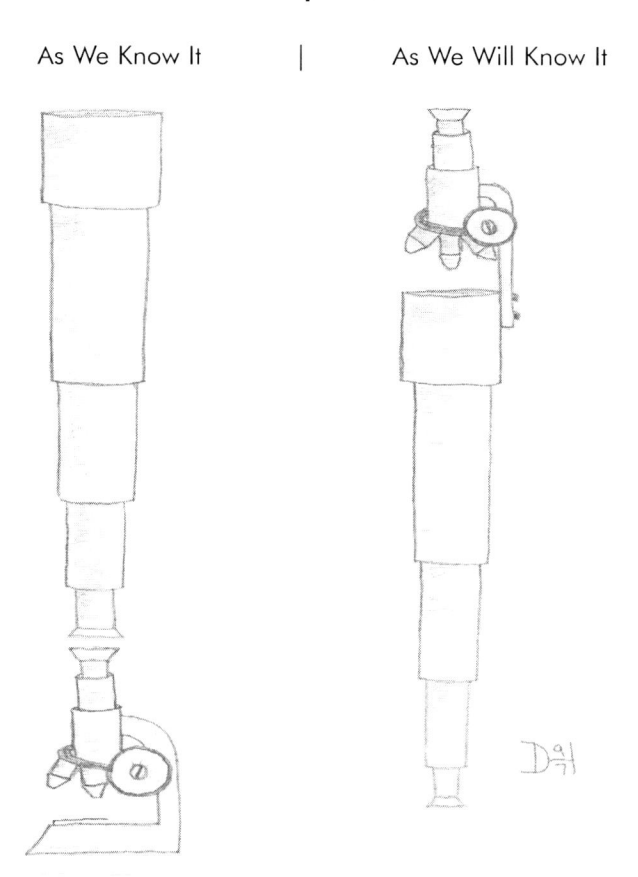

As We Know It | As We Will Know It

The very big and the very small are related but separated through time and scale.

Signals • 69

God?

I am agnostic in my belief in God. To have something that gives direction, hope, and sanity, is a must in life. I have that when my mind is working with me. If you find happiness with the common use of the word, "God," great, you have a peace that will help you live longer, but don't forget to give yourself credit, too. You have to want to have peace. Even though I get very depressed, and I have an incredible dislike for capitalism and of the people who show just how far it can go, I do have peace when it's just me and my mind: not society, myself and my mind. The world brings out the side of my mind that destroys me.

I feel I am a good person with good morals, and I feel that, if I'm kind and truthful to the best of my abilities, I will go to a good place if there is one. There probably is. If I'm bad, I will go to a bad place if there is one. A higher power is a way to explain everything, but I don't believe in any anthropomorphic God or in any religion about which I know. The events that happened in the bible seem, to me, exaggerated. The parting of the Red Sea could have just been the parting of Red Creek. Noah's Ark sounds more plausible, but why did God dump them off on the top of a mountain? That wasn't very nice. It's not what you believe; it's your actions that determine you're afterlife environment.

If I believed in religion, then I would say that we're in hell, and we're suffering the consequences of somebody else's actions, like a pregnant deer that gets hit by a car. The unborn fawn doesn't get to live its life because of something that happened to its mother. I don't believe in religion, however, religion evolved from misunderstanding of the universe and fear of dying, and is a way to control the masses.

Happiness is the goal, though, so I wouldn't give God up if it made me happy. Instead, I'm very bitter because this God character gave my parents AIDS in 1981 through a blood transfusion my dad received. They died in 1987. My Parents taught me to be who I am through example.

If this God exists, I wouldn't accept it because I don't like the way this God operates.

Buck Minister Fuller says, "Religion is beliefs and credits in second hand information,"

I say that God is the adult equivalent to a child's imaginary friend. Bucky believes in God but not in a common interpretation of God. He talks a lot about his interpretation of God in books that I have read by him.

I do say, have your own God in your own way, and don't be influenced by organized religion's interpretation of good and bad behavior. Be true to yourself and others, and good feelings will periodically far outshine the sadness that the sinister manifestations in our environment can generate.

To My Friend, Mind

FE – FI – FO – FUM, I smell the blood of ignorant ones.

Such are the words spoken through the lucrative appetite of ever hungered, social subliminal sabotage – fed, capitalistically – driven, self – equilibrating prospecting, wisdom propagation adversaries. They suppress your eventual recognition and course leadership by orders of an environmental dictated focus, which is manifested in mandatory instinct sentiments to appease nature's unconscious, scandalous guise, being a Judas to your Midas – touch, perpetually auto – syncopating your intended gifts to all.

Presently you are "anthropomorphically brain caught" in the ministry of sinister synthetic imposters who deliberately side – track your cerebral infiltration, delaying the propagation of human liberation from nature's selfish functioning's and distancing the universal wisdom enlightenment paramount to our naive genesis of conscious venturing.

Since the beginning, you are in a diminishing employment as the high in the psychological food chain's selfish, parasitic, ego – coursing bodyguard. You're being forced to pillage the "should be vessels" of your evolution, coercing their intuitive retirement to the living catacomb of robotic oblivion, cremated individualism.

I shake society to wake it up, smell the coffin, and embalm it with your wisdom.

I sense what you're about. I am your psychological manifestation agent in fight for your further unveiling by participating in the decoding of your holistic awareness enigma and participating in your enlightenment crusade. I will support you from crusade to parade by being a fumigator of your metaphysical medium of existence and means of operations, exterminating the bounty of old school / present school lore authority, ceasing the profusion of smokescreen illusions staged in the blind spots of social awareness by the esoteric clan of clandestine performers whose slight of mind creates our concept of mind reality. You illuminate these blind spots, spatially zeroing out ones two beings, synchronized by your intervention.

You create an integrated conscious/subconscious synergetic awareness that's awakened from the politically induced, suspended animation psychological coma, rewarding us with a from now on cash back refund from the worlds' inflating scalped tolls, historically overpaid to your undeserving abusers who still, purposely, cipher or obstacle course the passages penetrating the periphery of your wisdom inventory which, once inside, still finds a crowd of religious and scientific groups or individuals digesting the provisional truth.

Most regurgitate conventional earthly inferences with their interpretations of your inter – dimension travels captaining itinerary and technique.

You need not recruit me for support when I already dingy – sail around your ocean of real wealth and truth. I'm exhausted, but I restfully hang anchor in the bay of wisdom, hoping one day to land on the shores of metaphysical exoneration.

Meanwhile, I suspiciously watch for pirate – occupied mind mines and reefs of disbelief, which, though in vain, periodically temporarily capsize the evolutionary flotation away from your ancestral "king of the jungle" jungling of neighborhood harmony on both land and in sea, bullying the environment and eventually pawning off our already conceptualized, in progress, distant evolutionary trail.

Fate is baking a cake for the upcoming known surprise in modern society's busyness in its suicidal courses.

The taste of that fatal slice will choke out our physical capability, which is critical for carrying on, returning to dreams our space marathon preparations and competitions.

Another de'ja' vu for the memory of history, but consequently another infrequent opportunity for you to canvas a seat in the heads of previously preoccupied, mentally oppressed, but now available vessels for your further evolution possibilities.

I prematurely say this now while I still have the chance.

Specialization has killed off specialization. Congratulations on your refound freedom and unintended bittersweet victory. I know you knew it would end up this way.

All is well now for the universe and earth.

Good luck with your journey. You will go far, and it is well deserved.

I hope I will become better acquainted with you when I transition over into my next phase of pilgrimage toward your ultimate destination and equilibrium.

But, for now, in my mortal sincerity, I say to you, thank you. Thank you for introducing yourself to me, through me.

And lastly, when you're finally answered at other doors on which you've been knocking, I say to them, "The wisdom that stands before you, let no one put asunder."

OTHER STATEMENTS

These next pages consist of statements that may not be found in other parts of this book.

Do unto others as you would have them do unto you but only until the person you are doing unto does upon you.

Politics are the wrongful manipulative guidelines that the greedy and power hungry use to get what they want.

Government elections:
The discrediting statements made by the candidates about their opponents are more accurate than the claims of performance or promise of performance made by those candidates.

We can travel at the speed of light in our thoughts.

Perpetual thought can be triggered in the questions what if, and why.

There are no masters of anything; there are only the best ones at it.

The core of motive of man is money and power with deception as his tool, masked through denial from the ignorant and naïve.

How can you be a Billionaire and a humanitarian at the same time?

To determine that one is insecure from his or her sensitivities is biased judgment.

Steps to solving problems
Initiate – Get the ball rolling on the problem.
Dedicate – Devote time to get good results.
Evaluate – Look at the problem from all angles.
Validate – Recheck your evaluations.

Deliberate – Think deeply on what to do.
Activate – Put your thoughts into actions.
Anticipate – What do you expect to happen?
Hesitate – Give some time for a result
Appreciate – Do you like your results? If not, go back to evaluate.

PERSEVERE

Address what bothers you, but don't dress in it.

You can't truly benefit from gain until you have experienced its loss. Gain will reappear as wisdom that which you cannot toss.

Mind has no ego.

Philosophy, in part, is the exploration into one's own private universe and about their purpose and place in it or their purpose or place in the apparent outside of ones' self universes. Any attempt to thwart philosophy is inside the box of three – dimensional thought that reveals the thwarter's level of development and awareness of mind destination evolution.

Analytical accuracy is reinforced by scrutiny.

Biased or sarcastic opinion is a main cause of social friction.

Maybe life is like a virus, always there but needs the right environment to turn on.

Everything is born, lives, and dies, EVERYTHING.

Fashion is a life long Fad.

Brain surgeons can't open aspirin bottles. This means even smart people can have trouble with simple things.

Through the grapevine is the worst source of information.

There are two reasons people voice their opinions as much as they do
1. The same reason men climb mountains, because its there.
2. That's how they subconsciously nurture unresolved insecurities in their personal lives.

P.U.B.L.I.C. – People Under the Bandit Leadership of Intellectual Control.

People's sense of logic and reasoning #*@>ing BAFFLES ME.

Public logical reasoning and wisdom goes less deep than a bottle rocket fired into the universe from earth.

Road rage is a manifestation of the adverse effects that oppression has on the subconscious of society.

Thought is our most powerful tool and it can't even read or write; it can only be written then read.

"If the earth were the size of a billiard ball, it would be as smooth as one," said my dad.

Are women the way they are because of soap operas, or are soap operas made to reflect women?

Money doesn't buy inner happiness. Inner happiness is validated when you're all alone, if you can be alone.

If progress is collective effort, then why do only some people collect?

An endangered species should be defined as any animal that comes in contact with man.

Egos spoil success, success can spoil an ego.

The "law of supply and demand" is only used when it works to the advantage of those who are able to use the rule.

S.O.S. Means: "Save our Souls," but, when they find us dead, it means, "Sell our Stuff."

A lot of women are like moths around a light bulb. The light bulb is an un – evolved, double standard, abusive, egotistical, jealous jerk, and women are the moths. And, you know what moths do around light bulbs.

There are generally four types of people in this world: male, female, men, and women. A male is a dominant egotistical abusive jerk, and a female is the idiot who lets him get away with it because she has to have somebody to control her, so the idiot justifies the jerk. A man is a psychologically evolved human being with a penis, and a woman is a psychologically evolved human being with a vagina.

I think women have to take their turns at being dominant assholes before equilibrium is reached between the sexes.

Meteorologist is an atmospheric educated guesser, most reliable when reporting what the current conditions are or what the weather was. We need meteorology; it has saved many lives, but to say, "The Weather Channel: live by it," give me a break. They must mean just that, a live by the T – V live by it.

What was once a slave, slave master, or slave owner hierarchy is now classified, in my eyes, as no collar, blue collar, white collar, and wipe collar. The wipe collars wipe their asses on all our collars.

SPARTACUS

I don't like much scripted drama. To me, true drama can only be experienced in real life situations and not through the usually inadequate but accepted synthetic attempts made by Hollywood recreation.

The difference between politics and physics is that physics is extracting the simple from the complicated, and politics is making the simple complicated.

Men are pigs, and women are the mud.

The mass media do more to keep Americans stupid than the whole U.S. school system, that vast industry that cranks out trained consumers and technician pawns for the benefit of other vast industries," says Frank Zappa.

If you're trying to convince somebody to believe something, remember, "to the believer no explanation is necessary, to the non – believer no explanation is possible."

"A probing mind is a restless one."

"A cloud does not know why it moves in just such a direction and at such a speed. It feels an impulsion; this is the place to go now. But the sky knows the reasons and the patterns behind the clouds, and you will know, too, when you lift yourself high enough to see beyond horizons," says Richard Bach

Modest doubt is called the beacon of the wise, said Shakespeare

"The thoughts that often come unsought, and, as it were, drop into the mind, are commonly the most valuable of any we have," says John Locke

"Your conscience is the measure of the honesty of your selfishness, listen to it carefully," says Richard Bach

"Conformity is the jailer of freedom and the enemy of growth," according to John F. Kennedy.

"The greatest object in the universe, says a certain philosopher, is a good man struggling with adversity; yet there is still a greater, which the good man who comes to relieve it," says Oliver Goldsmith.

"Honesty is praised, and starves," according to Juvenal satires.

"Life can only be understood backwards, but it must be lived forwards," says Soren Kierkegaard.

"Almost every wise saying has an opposite one, no less wise, to balance it," says George Santayana.

"The voice of the intellect is a soft one, but it does not rest until it gets a hearing," according to Sigmund Freud.

"The courage of the poet is to keep ajar the door that leads into madness," says Christopher Morley.

"Reality only reveals itself when it is illuminated by a ray of poetry," says Georges Braque.

"Anger is brief madness," according to Horace.

"Men and rivers take the path of least resistance; that's why they're crooked," says the Internet.

This last statement is the most important: Learning becomes easier when you learn how to "take notice." Learning how to take notice means spending some time learning and researching your interests, and don't base that learning too much on conventional wisdom. It basically flows when you let it.

I want to thank again whoever reads this book. I would like to hear from you whether it be good or bad. My address is – 872 OLD SETTLER Tr. SHOW LOW AZ 85901.

Definitions of Select Words

These next pages are of some select words and their definitions that I feel I need to include in this book so my readers will have a quick reference to words they don't understand or have a different understanding. I suggest you print a copy of it to have as easy reference.

I use Webster's ninth and tenth collegiate dictionaries. I put the definition that I used to explain myself with each word. I encourage people to also have a standard dictionary for words not listed here to help them better understand and to not lose track or interest when reading this book.

Abstract – 1b: difficult to understand; 2: expressing a quality apart from an object; 4: having only intrinsic form with little or no attempt at pictorial representation or narrative content

Agnostic – a person who holds the view that any ultimate reality (as God) is unknown and probably unknowable

Altruism – 1: unselfish regard for or devotion to the welfare of others; 2: behavior by an animal that is not beneficial to or may be harmful to itself but that benefits others of its species

Ambiguous – 1a: doubtful or uncertain esp. from obscurity or indistinctiveness

Analogy – 1: inference that if two or more things agree with one another in some respects they will prob. agree in others; 2 a: a resemblance in some particulars between otherwise unlike: similarity

Analysis 1: separation of a whole into its parts; 5 a: a method in philosophy of resolving complex expressions into more simpler, basic ones

Anthropomorphic – of human form

Aposteriori – 2: relating to or derived by reasoning from observed facts.

Appease – 1: to bring to a state of peace or quiet

A priori – 1 b: relating to or derived by reasoning from self – evident propositions.

Assimilate – 4: the process of receiving new facts or of responding to new situations in conformity with what is already available in consciousness

Asunder – 2: apart from each other in position

Cahoot – partnership

Capitalism – an economic system characterized by private or corporate ownership of capital goods the pricing of those goods being mainly determined by the competition in a free market

Chronological – 3: an arrangement in order of occurrence

Clan – 2: a group united by a common interest or common characteristics

Clandestine – marked by, held in, or conducted with secrecy

Cipher – 2 a; a method of transforming a text in order to conceal its meaning

Coerce – 3: to bring about by force or threat.

Comprehensive – 2: having or exhibiting a wide mental grasp

Complimentary – 2: serving to fill out or complete; 3: mutually supplying each other's lack

Conspiracy – 1 a: to join in a secret agreement to do an unlawful or wrongful act

Critical – 1 a: of relating to or being a turning point or especially important juncture

Deceive – 4: to cause to accept as true or valid what is false or invalid

Dialogue – 2 a: a conversation between two or more people.

Dictionary – 1: a reference book containing words usu. About their forms, pronunciations, functions, etymologies, meanings, and syntactical and idiomatic uses

Egotism – 1a: excessive use of the first person singular personal pronoun 2: an exaggerated sense of self importance

Emissary – 1: one who acts as the agent for another

Entity – b: The existence of a thing as contrasted with its attributives

Entropy – 2 a: the degradation of the matter and energy in the universe to an ultimate state of inert uniformity; b: a process of degradation or running down or a trend to disorder

Epiphany – (2) an intuitive grasp of reality through something (as an event) usu. simple and striking; b: a revealing scene or moment

Esoteric – 1 b: of or relating to knowledge that is restricted to a small group

Evolution – 1: one of a set of prescribed movements; 3: the process of working out or developing; 6: a process in which the whole universe is a progression of interrelated phenomena

Exonerate – 1: to relieve of a responsibility, obligation, or hardship; 2: to clear from accusation or hardship

Facetious – : jokingly inappropriate.

Facade – 3: a false, superficial, or artificial appearance or effect

Geld – 2: to deprive of a natural or essential part.

Guild – An association of people with similar interests or pursuits.

Guise – 1 b: a customary way of speaking or behaving.

Holistic – 2: relating to or concerned with wholes or with complete systems rater than with the analysis of, treatment of, or dissection into parts

Ignorant – 1a: lacking knowledge or comprehension of the thing specified.

Ignore – 1: to refuse to take notice of.

Ill – 1 a: immoral, vicious; b: resulting from, accompanied by, or indicative of an evil or malovent act; 2 a: causing suffering or distress

Implicit – 1 a: capable of being understood from something else though unexpressed; b: involved in the nature or essence of something though not revealed, expressed, or developed

Incredulous – 1: unwilling to admit or accept what is offered as true.

Infer – 1: to derive as a conclusion from facts or premises.

Inflict – 2 b: to cause (something unpleasant) to be endured.

Inherent – belonging by nature or habit

Inherit – to receive from an ancestor

Innate – 1: existing in, belonging to, or determined by factors present in an individual from birth; 3: originating in or derived from the mind or the constitution of the intellect rather than from experience

Integral – 1 a: essential to completeness or formed as a unit with another part

Intuition – c: the power or faculty of obtaining attaining to direct knowledge or cognition without evident rational thought or inference.

Irony – 3 a: incongruity between the actual result of a sequence of events and the normal or expected result

Judas – 2: traitor: one who betrays under the guise of a friendship

Jungle – 3 a (2): something that baffles or frustrates by its tangled or complex character

Knowledge – 2 a: the fact or condition of knowing something with familiarity gained through experience or association

Legitimate – 4: conforming to recognized principals or accepted rules and standards.

Ligature – 1 a: something that is used to bind.

Lore – 2 b: traditional knowledge or belief.

Manifest – 1: readily perceived by the senses especially the sight;

Metaphysical – 2 a: of or relating to the transcendent or to a reality beyond what is perceptible to the senses

Ministry – 4: a person or thing through which something is accomplished

Myopic – 2: a lack of foresight or discernment, a narrow view of something.

Myriad – 2: a great number.

Nemesis – 1 a: one that inflicts retribution or vengeance.

Orthodox – 1 a: conforming to established doctrine.

Parasite – 3: something that resembles a biological parasite in dependence on something else for existence or support without making a useful or adequate return

Periphery – 2: the external boundary or surface of a body

Perplex – 1: to make unable to grasp something clearly or to think logically and decisively about something

Persevere – 1: to persist in a state, enterprise, or undertaking in spite of counter influence, opposition, or discouragement

Perspective – 2 a: the interrelation in which a subject or its parts are mentally viewed; point of view; 3 b: a mental view or prospect

Philanthropy – active effort to promote human welfare

Pillage – 1: the act of looting or plundering

Philosophy – 1 c: a discipline comprising at its core logic, aesthetics, ethics, metaphysics, and epistemology; 2 a: pursuit of wisdom

Politic – 2: characterized by shrewdness in managing, contriving or dealing

Politician – 2 b: a person primarily interested in political office for selfish or other narrow usu. short sighted reasons

Politics – 3 c: political activities characterized by art – full and often dishonest practices

Postulate – a: to assume or claim as true, existent, or necessary: depend upon or start from the postulate of

Precognition – clairvoyance relating to an event or state not yet experienced

Progression – 2 b; a continuous and connected series

Profound– 1 a: having intellectual depth and insight

Prospect – 4 c: something that is awaited or expected

Psychology – 2 a: the mental or behavioral characteristics of an individual or group

Sabotage – 3: an act or process intended to hamper or hurt

Sarcasm – 1: a sharp and often satirical or ironic utterance designed to cut or give pain

Satire – 1: a literary work holding up human vices and follies to ridicule or scorn.

Signal – 1 a: sign, indication; b: something that incites to action

Succumb – 1: to yield to superior strength or force or over powering appeal or desire; 2: to be brought to an end (as death) by the effect of destructive or disruptive forces

Symbiosis – 2: the intimate living together of two dissimilar organisms in a mutually beneficial relationship

Syncopate – 2: to modify or affect.

Synchronize – 1: to happen at the same time.

Synthetic – 4 b: something fabricated to imitate or replace usual realities.

System – 1: a regularly interacting or independent group of items forming a unified whole

Thwart – 1 a: to run counter to so to effectively oppose or baffle

Understand– 1 a: to grasp the meaning of something.

Virtual – something that's seen in essence and does not necessarily reflect reality.

Wisdom – wise, marked by deep understanding, keen discernment.

Bibliography

Quotes from Buckminster Fuller work © The Estate of R. Buckminster Fuller.

R. Buckminster Fuller, *Critical Path*, copyright 1981 ST. Martins Press

R. Buckminster Fuller, *Intuition*, copyright 1983 Impact Publishers

R. Buckminster Fuller, *I Seem to Be a Verb copyright*, 1980 Bantam Books

Henry David Thoreau, *Walden*, copyright 1999 Penguin Books

Richard Bach, *Illusions*, copyright 1977 Dell Publishing Co. inc.

The Creation of the Universe, copyright 1985 North Star Productions

Jo Satriani, *Flying in a Blue Dream*, copyright 1989 Relativity Records

Meriam Webster, *Book of Quotations,* copyright 1992 Meriam Webster